"I love this book because its title delivers. To be able to explain what the gospel is, how it works in our own lives, and how it's shared is a unique and powerful combination I've never seen before. Jeff has written a book that will be around a long time because it reforms evangelism in a fresh way."

> **Bob Roberts,** Senior Pastor, Northwood Church; author, *Bold as Love* and *Lessons from the East*

"Jeff calls us back to the gospel, not as a trite phrase to throw around in Christian circles but as a life-changing language in which we grow more fluent as we use it in community. The analogy to learning a foreign language helps us envision how to become fluent in the gospel, working, eating, and even dreaming while immersed in the good news of Jesus and how that changes everything. This is an extremely practical and helpful book!"

> **Wendy Alsup,** teacher; blogger; author, *Is the Bible Good for Women?* and *Practical Theology for Women*

"It's easy to forget how good the good news of the gospel is. This practical book will help you to see that good news, and to share it with others."

> **Russell Moore,** President, Ethics & Religious Liberty Commission of the Southern Baptist Convention

"Even the title of this book, *Gospel Fluency*, gets at a right understanding of the gospel: the message from God that must be spoken. Our communication of the gospel is more than a data dump; it's a message that we must share without accent, as native speakers who have immersed themselves in knowing and speaking the living gospel. Jeff's clear call, through compelling stories and biblical foundations, is to connect the gospel to all areas of life, and then speak it fluently to believers and nonbelievers alike."

> **J. Mack Stiles,** author, *Evangelism: How the Whole Church Speaks of Jesus* and *Marks of the Messenger*

"Jeff Vanderstelt has a gift for clarifying and simplifying what is often complex and puzzling. *Gospel Fluency* is no exception. In this book, Jeff invites believers, unbelievers, pastors, and church leaders to think about their faith with fresh eyes and fresh language. He invites us not to a system, a catchphrase, or a fad, but to a refreshing vision of Christ our Savior and the life he offers."

> **Mike Cosper,** Pastor of Worship and Arts, Sojourn Community Church, Louisville, Kentucky

"I have known Jeff for over a decade now, and his heart beats for the church to be all that God has called her to be in Christ. He is not just an ideas man; he is on the ground, living out the truths you read in this book. As the culture shifts and attractional ministry fades, Jeff will be a faithful guide for us all."

Matt Chandler, Lead Pastor, The Village Church, Dallas, Texas; President, Acts 29 Church Planting Network; author, *The Mingling of Souls* and *The Explicit Gospel*

"When Christians speak about the gospel, it should sound like our native tongue. *Gospel Fluency* helps us articulate and live the gospel we love. Our 'fluency' in the gospel is necessary for us to be ambassadors for our gospel-giving King. We need books like *Gospel Fluency* to both ground us in our practice of the gospel and raise us out of living our daily lives in the cultural drift."

Daniel Montgomery, Lead Pastor, Sojourn Community Church, Louisville, Kentucky; Founder, Sojourn Network; coauthor, *Faithmapping, PROOF,* and *Leadership Mosaic*

"I've been wanting to have a resource from Jeff on this topic for a very long time. It is so, so, so needed. As I've worked with different Christians from several churches around the city of Chicago, I've witnessed the lack of gospel understanding that has permeated many 'solid' churches. I will personally hand out copies of this book like gospel tracts."

Jackie Hill Perry, poet; writer; hip-hop artist

Gospel Fluency

GOSPEL FLUENCY

Speaking the Truths of Jesus into
the Everyday Stuff of Life

JEFF VANDERSTELT

WHEATON, ILLINOIS

Library of Congress Cataloging-in-Publication Data

Names: Vanderstelt, Jeff, 1969– author.
Title: Gospel fluency : speaking the truths of Jesus into the everyday stuff of life / Jeff Vanderstelt ; foreword by Jackie Hill Perry.
Description: Wheaton, Illinois : Crossway, 2017. | Includes bibliographical references and index. | Description based on print version record and CIP data provided by publisher; resource not viewed.
Identifiers: LCCN 2016035974 (print) | LCCN 2016028971 (ebook) | ISBN 9781433546044 (pdf) | ISBN 9781433546051 (mobi) | ISBN 9781433546068 (epub) | ISBN 9781433546037 (hc)
Subjects: LCSH: Christian life. | Christian life—Biblical teaching.
Classification: LCC BV4501.3 (print) | LCC BV4501.3 .V3655 2017 (ebook) | DDC 248.4—dc23
LC record available at https://lccn.loc.gov/2016035974

To

Jayne, my friend, bride, and partner for life.
Your faith inspires me. Your wisdom helps me.
Your love for Jesus has changed me.

Haylee, Caleb, and Maggie.
You make me smile, laugh, cry, and pray.
You are making me more like Jesus.
I pray you continue to become more like him as well.

Doxa Church.
Thank you for embracing the Vanderstelts as family.
I regularly thank God for all of you.
You are so dear to my heart.

The Soma Family of Churches.
You have become more than I ever dreamed
and encourage me more than you know.
You truly are family.
I love you.

Contents

PART 4: THE GOSPEL WITH US

PART 5: THE GOSPEL TO OTHERS

Foreword

The book you are holding is very important. Why? Because it has the potential to save your life.

Every human being on earth needs salvation, not only from the wrath to come, but also from the flimsy theology permeating our Christian communities. That might sound a bit extreme, but in essence it is true. The good news has been demoted to the position of Easter Sunday sermons and altar calls, while sin and discouragement wreak havoc in the inner workings of those sitting in the pews.

If you were to ask many Christians what the gospel is, the answers would sing a tune of Christ's life, death, burial, and resurrection. The accuracy of these answers would leave you to assume that there is application—until you pose a follow-up question, such as, "How do you apply the gospel to the everyday stuff of life?" Then blank stares and fumbling words would reveal the disconnect many Christians have between the gospel and its power not only to save our souls but also to change our lives.

I believe that what you are holding in your hand can be the catalyst for such change.

Though its contents may bring about fresh ideas, I assure you that it is not rooted in anything new. To the contrary, this book follows in the footsteps of the apostles by delivering to you what is of first importance (1 Cor. 15:3), that is, the good news of Jesus Christ.

I personally have been greatly impacted by the gospel-saturated ministry of Jeff Vanderstelt. His emphasis on gospel fluency has shaped everything from my poetry to my music and even the way I discipline my one-year-old. There have been many occasions when I've found her splattering juice around the kitchen floor like a miniature Jackson Pollock, and I've thought, "How I respond in this moment will lay the foundation for how she understands grace and the gospel."

Though she's too young to understand now, the principle is still very pertinent. The gospel should impact us not just theologically but also practically. From our preaching to our parenting, the good news gives us the blueprint for how to function within these spheres in a way that glorifies Christ.

I believe that is why gospel fluency must first take root in our hearts before we can expect it to blossom in our respective ministries. Whether it is motherhood or missions, I have realized that if I am not gospel fluent in my thought life, then I won't be in my speech. If I am not gospel fluent in my speech, then I won't be in my evangelism or my discipleship. I have come across many godly men and women who are walking through life with the people in their churches by teaching them how to study Scripture, helping them understand spiritual disciplines, finances, relationships, and so on. Yet the deceptive blind spot in their discipleship relationships is that they have discipled people in how to successfully do all of the above *without* Christ. Oh, how easy it is to create women and men in *our* image, who are living morally correct lives while being gospel deficient. We do a great disservice to the people God has called us to disciple if we disciple them into anything other than Christ.

Being gospel fluent inevitably shapes how we live, which then affects how we engage with the world around us. This is why this book is so profoundly necessary. It will cause us to get back to the basics of Christianity, where the good news *is* good news again; where the beautiful reminder of what God did for us in Christ can break through the chaos and usher us into the love of God; where the gospel isn't an appendix to a sermon but the mountain on which all preaching stands; and where we can recognize that the gospel doesn't just save us but *keeps* us.

Jackie Hill Perry

Acknowledgments

First, I have to thank Justin Taylor for continuing to push me toward writing *Gospel Fluency*. Although *Saturate* was my first book, Justin has gently prodded me to write this book for many years now. He blogged about my training on gospel fluency, sent out countless tweets, and regularly asked if I was ever going to put it into print. He made sure that it happened, just as he ensured that I published this book with Crossway. He did it because he believed that this work would serve many, and I earnestly pray it does.

I also must acknowledge how Josh McPherson and the Grace Community Church family in Wenatchee, WA, contributed to this work. Years ago, Josh and the GCC family provided me places to get away and write because they believed this book would greatly serve the church. Thank you, Josh and GCC, for making the space to break my writing ground that eventually led to my finishing *Gospel Fluency*.

And I likely never would have started writing if Sealy Yates, my agent, hadn't listened to two of his authors, who told him to go after me. Thank you, Sealy, for encouraging me to get the initial book proposal out to publishers and for connecting me to the Crossway team that has been such a blessing to me in this process.

Thank you, Greg Bailey, for editing both *Gospel Fluency* and *Saturate*. You have made my work better.

Abe Meysenburg and Randy Sheets, next to Jayne, you are my two faithful friends, who never hesitate to proclaim the gospel to my unbelief and build me up with the gospel in my despairing moments. I have grown in Christ immensely because both of you speak the gospel to me. You are true friends.

I also want to thank Amy Lathrop, Rachel Northey, and Sara Parker, who read many versions of this book as it was being written, providing great feedback while also encouraging me not to give up when I had bad writing days.

I am deeply indebted to Tim Keller for the profound influence he has had on my life, mostly from afar through his preaching, training, and writing. I am certain that I would not be as gospel fluent myself if I had not learned so much from Tim. Other than Jesus Christ, Tim's life and work have had more impact on *Gospel Fluency* than anyone or anything.

Of course, it is to Jesus, my Savior and Lord, I am most indebted for eternity. I love you, Jesus, and will forever live to display and declare your glory. You deserve more than any of us will ever give you, and because of that, I, along with countless others, will spend eternity singing, proclaiming, and displaying your praise! You are worthy of all praise, glory, and honor—my King, my Savior, my Lord, and my Friend.

PART 1

GOSPEL FLUENCY

1

EVERYONE IS AN UNBELIEVER

I'm an unbeliever. So are you.

"*Wait*," you're thinking. "What are you doing writing a book about the gospel of Jesus Christ if you're an unbeliever? And what do you know about me? Who do you think I am?"

I grew up believing that people fall into two categories: you are either a believer or an unbeliever; you either believe in Jesus Christ and what he has done for us or you don't. Now, after more than twenty-five years as a pastor, I see that every one of us is an unbeliever, including me—at least in some areas of our lives.

Don't misunderstand me. I do believe there are some who are regenerate children of God and others who are not yet.

There are those who have been given new life through faith in Jesus. They have become new creations and have been given fresh starts because of their faith in Jesus Christ and what he has done for them. And I believe there are others who are still dead in their sins and not yet truly alive in Christ (see John 1:12–13; 2 Cor. 5:17; Eph. 2:1–10).

When I say we are all unbelievers, I mean we still have places in our lives where we don't believe God. There are spaces where we don't trust his word and don't believe that what he accomplished in Jesus Christ is enough to deal with our past or what we are facing in this moment or the next.

We don't believe his word is true or his work is sufficient.

We don't believe. We are unbelievers.

I struggle with unbelief on a daily basis. I have a conversation with my wife, and when she points out something I've yet to get better at, I hear the word *failure* in my head.

I try to lead a good conversation about the Bible at the dinner table with my children, but instead of eager beavers on the edges of their seats, I get slouched bodies and rolling eyes. *Bad father.*

I teach on being a good neighbor, one who knows the stories of the people who live on your street, but since I moved into my current neighborhood a few months ago, I know only the story of failed attempts to meet people. *Hypocrite.*

Unbelief.

I slip in and out of believing God's word about me and trusting in his work for me. Jesus gave his life to make me a new creation. He died to forgive me of my sins and change my identity from *sinner* to *saint*, from *failure* to *faithful*, and from *bad* to *good* and even *righteous* and *holy*. But I forget what he has said about me. I forget what he has done for me. And sometimes it isn't forgetfulness. Sometimes it's just plain unbelief. I know these things. I just don't believe them.

I am an unbeliever. Not every moment, of course. But I have those moments.

So do you. I'm certain of it.

We all struggle with unbelief in God because the message of who he is and what he has done for us can sound unbelievable at times. We all slip in and out of confidence that what he has done for us in Jesus is sufficient for us today.

It's very possible that even though you are familiar with Jesus, you have yet to believe in him for yourself, for your life. Or maybe you have come to faith in Jesus, but it hasn't really changed what you do daily or how you engage in the everyday stuff of life.

The apostle Paul said to the believers in Jesus in Galatia, "The life I now live in the flesh I live by faith in the Son of God [Jesus], who loved me and gave himself for me" (Gal. 2:20). They had started with faith in Jesus, but they were putting their faith and hope in something else to make them right instead of Jesus. Paul called them back to an awareness that the good news about Jesus—the gospel—is for all of life: everything.

A life of true living is a life of faith in Jesus, a life of believing in Jesus in the everyday stuff of life.

I'm still learning how to live like that. I'm still an unbeliever in many ways. And yet, I don't want to stay that way. I want all of my life to be marked by faith in Jesus.

God is intent on making everything about Jesus because it is *through him* that all things came into existence and it is *in him* that they are sustained (Eph. 1:22–23; Col. 1:15–20).

God also wants to rescue you from unbelief and sanctify you to become like Jesus. *Sanctification* is just a big word for becoming more and more *like* Jesus through faith *in* Jesus. You *become like* what you *believe in*. So becoming like Jesus requires believing in him more and more in every part of your

life. Sanctification is moving from unbelief in Jesus to belief in
him in the everyday stuff of life.

You're not there yet, are you? Neither am I. We're still unbelievers who need Jesus more—in more ways and more places.
As I wrote this book, I came to see once again how badly
I need Jesus. Sometimes I believed my writing could change a
life. But when a writing day went poorly, I was crushed under
the weight of this responsibility. I needed to believe again that
God changes lives, not me.

Sure, he works through us to do it, but he isn't dependent
on how well we do it. God can speak through anyone and
anything. He actually spoke through a donkey once (in the
older versions of the Bible, a different word was used in place
of *donkey*.) So I guess he can speak through me.

Remembering this, I went from unbelief to belief. "Jeff," I
said to myself (or others said to me when I forgot), "trust in
God's work, not yours. Believe in his words spoken over your life
through Jesus, not yours." Then I could rest again while I wrote.

So I kept writing as the fruit of my faith in Jesus.

This doesn't just happen for me when I write. I find myself
needing to do this when I have to get up early to work out; consider how we are going to pay the bills; or sit in the Interstate
405 parking lot that we call a highway, but which so often isn't
moving when I need to be someplace sooner than everyone else
on the road!

I need to remember because I forget. I need to believe because I don't.

Thankfully, I don't do this alone. I have a community of
people around me who are also professing unbelievers. They
believe in Jesus, but not all the time for everything. Not yet,
at least.

We are journeying together, moving from unbelief to belief
in Jesus more each day—and sometimes less the next day.

That is why I am writing this book. I know that I need this book, and so do you.

We all face daily struggles and battles, sometimes from enemies we can't even see. We hear lies and accusations. We struggle with temptations and we are often deceived. We hear words that were spoken over us when we were younger, echoing in our hearts in ways that don't breed life to our souls. We look at our present situations and wish they were better. And many of us face uncertain futures that, without God, cause us to lead lives of anxiety, worry, and fear.

We all need help because we can come up with plenty of reasons not to believe, not to hope, and not to trust in God's word and work for us.

We need the gospel and we need to become gospel-fluent people. We need to know how to believe and speak the truths of the gospel—the good news of God—in and into the everyday stuff of life. In other words, we need to know how to address the struggles of life and the everyday activities we engage in with what is true of Jesus: the truths of what he accomplished through his life, death, and resurrection, and, as a result, what is true of us as we put our faith in him. The gospel has the power to affect everything in our lives.

I wrote this book because I love unbelievers and I know God does too. He loves you and wants to save you from your unbelief.

I believe the only hope for all of us is the gospel of Jesus Christ and communities that live life together while proclaiming this gospel into one another's lives daily—gospel-fluent communities.

Jesus said we are to make disciples who can make disciples (see Matt. 28:18–20), and a disciple of Jesus should know, believe, and be able to speak the gospel. He or she also should be capable of leading others to know, believe, and speak the gospel.

My hope is that this book, first of all, will bring about hope and healing for you as you come to believe and apply the truths of the gospel to your life. I also hope that you and others around you will become fluent in the gospel, so that together you will be able to lead others to find hope and help in Jesus in every part of their lives.

I am more certain than ever that apart from belief in the gospel, sinners will suffer everlasting punishment and saints will fail to live lives that bring glory and honor to Jesus Christ.

So it is my hope that more sinners will be saved from condemnation and more saints will be set free to overcome sin, fear, and insecurity in their everyday existence.

I hope that this book moves you from unbelief to more belief in the gospel of Jesus Christ and equips you to help others do the same.

2

GIVE THEM JESUS

"He's such a jerk! He's doing it again," Alisa said.

"What's he doing?" one of the members in our group asked.

"He's doing what he always does—canceling at the last minute when it's his turn to pick up the kids for the weekend. And then, when I talk to him about it, he intimidates and tries to threaten me. He scares me. And now I'm constantly thinking about how we're going to make it financially if he doesn't help us. Half the time, I don't want the kids to be with him, but I know they need to see their father. I don't want to see him or even talk to him. He's so intimidating! I just can't keep doing this. I'm constantly worrying and can hardly sleep."

Alisa's husband had cheated on her with her best friend.

Subsequently, the marriage had ended in a divorce. Neither of them was a believer in Jesus. Additionally, shortly after the affair, Alisa's house had been destroyed in a fire, and she had lost everything.

Alisa was introduced to our community when Clay and Kristie, new Christians and members of our missional community, asked if we'd be willing to help her. They knew Alisa through a mutual friend, and our kids all attended the same elementary school. Without a husband or a home, it was clear Alisa needed the help of God's family.

So we pitched in together to buy groceries and to provide money for her to purchase clothes and other necessary items. For a season, she and her two daughters lived with Clay and Kristie and their two children, Emma and Keagan. Eventually, Alisa started to hang out with our missional community and started learning about Jesus with us.

"Don't worry," one of the men in our group spoke up. "We'll take care of him! We're not going to let him treat you like this."

Someone else chimed in: "Alisa, you can't put up with this! You've got to stand up to him. And if you won't, we will. We won't just stand by and watch this happen to you."

The conversation continued like this for some time until I realized what was going on.

"Wait a minute, everyone!" I said. "This isn't what Alisa needs right now. She doesn't need us to make this about her husband any more than it already is."

I knew much of her problem had to do with the fact that she had already allowed her husband to have too much influence over her. He had taken center stage in her life to the point where she was emotionally controlled by his every behavior. In a sense, he had become her god.

I went on to say: "All we're doing is affirming him as the

problem. We're making the focus all about getting him to change. Sure, what he's doing is wrong. But we can't make this all about him. What if he never changes? Then Alisa will continue to be a slave to his brokenness. We can't change him. Alisa can't either. Only God can do that."

Alisa needed us to direct her to God for help. She needed something much better at the center of her life and attention—someone who could truly set her free and change her from the inside out. So I said: "We need to give Alisa Jesus, not our efforts to change her ex-husband. I'm not saying that we shouldn't have a conversation with him at some point, or that we shouldn't step in to protect her. However, let's start with Jesus first."

I turned to Alisa, saying: "You need Jesus to help you overcome your fear. You need Jesus to be your source of security and love. In fact, you also need Jesus to enable you to forgive and love your ex-husband."

I've seen this pattern play out many times over the years. I've been guilty of it myself. People share their struggles and, with every good intention, others give good advice or try to step in to be the solution themselves. People do need answers. They are in need of help. But we fail to truly help them if we don't give them Jesus. He is the best answer and the most powerful help they can receive.

Speak the Truth

The apostle Paul, in his letter to the church in Ephesus, states: "And he gave the apostles, the prophets, the evangelists, the shepherds and teachers, to equip the saints for the work of ministry, for building up the body of Christ, until we all attain to the unity of the faith and of the knowledge of the Son of God, to mature manhood, to the measure of the stature of the fullness of Christ, so that we may no longer be children, tossed to and fro by the waves and carried about by every wind of doctrine, by human cunning, by craftiness in deceitful schemes. *Rather, speaking the truth in love, we are to grow up in every way into him who is the head, into Christ"* (Eph. 4:11–15).

It is God's intent that every person who comes into a relationship with him through Jesus Christ eventually will grow up into maturity. And maturity looks like Jesus. He is the perfect human, providing an example of what we are meant to be. A mature Christian is one who resembles Jesus Christ in thought, attitude, emotion, and behavior. And one of the most significant ways by which we grow up into maturity is by speaking the truth in love to one another.

Many wrongly believe that speaking the truth in love is actually just speaking hard words to one another with loving hearts: "You have bad breath, but since I love you, I've got to speak the truth to you." "We want you in our group, but you aren't very kind to others, and as a result, people don't want to be around you! I'm just speaking the truth in love." But that is not what Paul is talking about here. Sure, we do need to speak truthfully to one another and do it with love, but Paul has something more in mind.

We need to read just a few verses further to discover what Paul means. He clarifies the truth that we are to speak to one another in verse 21. He states, "The truth is in Jesus." "Speaking the truth in love," for Paul, is shorthand for "speaking what is true about Jesus" to one another—that is, speaking the gospel to one another. Paul knows that if people are going to grow up *into* Christ in *every* way, they need to hear the *truths* of Jesus (the gospel) and learn to speak them *into everything*.

As my friends Steve Timmis and Tim Chester like to say: *"What's the question? Jesus is the answer. What's the problem? Jesus is the solution."*

Too often, when giving people answers to their questions or

solutions to their problems, we give them something other than Jesus. If they are struggling with their finances, we give them the best budgeting plans we know of. If they are working through relational discord, we teach them communication techniques. If they are struggling with doubt, we challenge them to just believe, promising that all will get better if they do.

But we fail if we don't give them Jesus.

In some cases, we encourage them to read their Bibles or pray, which, of course, are wonderful things. However, if we don't teach them to meet and know Jesus through their Bible reading and prayer, we are dangerously close to leading them away from Jesus through very good things. This is the heart of idolatry—taking a good thing and making it a "god thing." We take something God gave us to direct us to him and love it or depend on it more than him. As a result, we fail to come to him through it.

Missing Jesus

The religious leaders in Jesus's day were the greatest Bible scholars and the most religious pray-ers. Yet they completely missed Jesus! At one point, Jesus said to them, "You search the Scriptures because you think that in them you have eternal life; and it is they that bear witness about me, yet you refuse to come to me that you may have life" (John 5:39–40). They loved the Scriptures that point to Jesus, but didn't love and depend on Jesus. They missed the entire point!

I have met too many people who love their Bibles yet have no genuine relationship with Jesus Christ. They don't really know him. They don't really love him. They don't really worship him. Instead, they worship their Bibles. They are not growing up into maturity because they are not growing up into Christ.

Bible studies are great. Prayer is wonderful. Applying wisdom for financial planning, relationship building, and every other area of life is important and necessary. However, if we fail to give one another Jesus, we lead one another away from him. We might grow in Bible knowledge, but not in love for Jesus. We might become the most religious pray-ers of all and yet be talking to the wrong god. We could have our finances in order while our hearts are completely out of order because we are doing it all for the wrong reasons. We might be great at communication and conflict resolution, but if we are not reconciled with God through Jesus Christ, then our relationships will be shallow and temporary in nature.

Think of it this way: if we are to help one another grow up into Christ in every way, we need to learn how to speak the truths of Christ into everything—every aspect of life, every situation we face, and every issue we address.

What does the gospel of Jesus Christ teach us about our finances? How should we address relational discord in light of the gospel? How does what we know about Jesus shape how we handle anxiety and fear? If we speak the truths about Jesus into each of these issues or situations, we will grow up together in every way *with* Christ, which also means we will grow up in every way *into* Christ.

In other words, if we are going to grow up to be like Christ, we have to grow up with the very truths of Jesus.

However, if we try to instruct, counsel, or grow one another with something other than the truths of Jesus Christ, then every area in which we speak something other than Christ will be an area in which we grow away from him. This is why so many people look to Jesus only for their afterlife; they've been given the truths of Jesus primarily as the answer for going to heaven when they die. But they have little knowledge of how Jesus gives a better answer for what they do with their money, their sexuality, their work, or their families. Jesus is good news to them for their afterlife, but they wrongly believe he has little to nothing to offer them in the everyday stuff of life.

But he has truth to offer—for everything. He *has* better truth and he *is* better truth.

Jesus is the true and better human, and everything in life is better if Jesus is brought into it. He has done everything better. He can make everything better. And the truths about who he is and what he has done, when applied to our lives, are always a better answer than anything else. There is good news and great help for absolutely everything in life in the person and work of Jesus Christ.

Jesus and Sex

For instance, let's consider our sexuality. I remember hearing people say, when I was growing up, "You should wait until you're married to have sex because sex is always better if you wait."

Well, first of all, that isn't entirely true. As a married man, I have found that sex gets better the more you do it. Seriously, that's just true.

In fact, I tell most of the couples who come to me for premarital counseling that their first night together will likely include the worst sex they will ever have, but that it will get better with practice. Not that the wedding night will be bad. Engaging in sexual intercourse with one person to whom you've committed yourself for a lifetime is an amazingly sacred and enjoyable experience. It is God's very good and right plan that sexual intimacy be reserved for marriage.

However, the motive for abstinence is not better sex in the future. In fact, this motivation leads to the opposite experience. Why? Well, if your primary reason for waiting to engage in sexual intimacy is your own satisfaction, you undermine the purpose for sexual intimacy. The purpose is not the fulfillment of your selfish desires. In fact, most of the marriage problems I encounter in counseling spouses have to do with the faulty mind-set that marriage is all about them and their desires being fulfilled. Couples in the best marriages understand that giving yourself to another to please him or her glorifies God, satisfies the other, and brings great personal joy as well. Great marriages are self-giving, not self-serving.

How do I know this? Because sex and love were created by God, and Jesus showed us, in his life and death, how best to love.

So what reason should we give people to abstain from sexual activity prior to marriage?

Give them Jesus.

Tell them that the picture God has given us of his love for his people is that of a husband pursuing his bride. God loved his bride so much that he pursued her faithfully for hundreds of years. Eventually, God took on flesh in the form of a baby named Jesus, and he humbly lived as a human for thirty-three years. The writer of Hebrews says that Jesus is able to sympathize with our weaknesses because he was tempted in every way just as we are, yet he did not sin (Heb. 4:15). He fully understands us, the church, his bride, because he put himself in our shoes. Therefore, he is able to live with his bride in an understanding way, just as Peter directs husbands to do (1 Pet. 3:7). Jesus really knows his bride, so he really empathizes with her. He gets her better than any man has ever understood a woman!

Jesus loved his bride enough to serve her and give up his life as a ransom for her. She was unfaithful to him. She gave herself to others. She did not wait for him, but grew impatient and easily gave in to those not committed to a covenant relationship. And yet, he paid the bride price of his own life to purchase her out of her adulterous enslavement. His death on the cross paid the debt for her sin and cleansed her of all her impurities. With his own life, he purchased for her a perfectly pure wedding dress. In fact, the dress she gets to wear is his own righteousness, which covers the shame of her sin. He died to give her freedom, purity, and unending love. Then he rose again and went to prepare a place for her. One day, he will come for his bride and take her home to dwell with him forever. And though it has been more than two thousand years, he is patiently waiting for that day when his bride will be fully prepared, and he will consummate the marriage at the greatest wedding party of all eternity. He has been waiting faithfully all this time for his bride. Talk about a faithful, loving, and patient lover who is willing to wait for the love of his life!

The reason we wait to have sex until we are married is because of Jesus's faithfulness to us. We are his bride, and we live to tell the story of his love for us.

Jesus purchased our lives so that they would display his pure, holy, selfless, unadulterated love for us! And if we fail—*when* we fail—we remember God's love for us and run back to the cross in faith, trusting that Jesus died for us. We believe that his death paid for our sin and cleansed us from all unrighteousness; that we are now clothed in his righteousness; that we are changed; that we are new; and that God has declared us pure through the pure love of Jesus Christ.

This doesn't just change who we are. It changes how we live.

Because of Jesus's pure love for us, we want to tell the story of his love by displaying it through our own sexual purity. We want to be sexually pure not for selfish motives but for godly reasons: we want the world to know that though we have betrayed the love of our life, we have been forgiven and made new, and he has not forsaken us because of what we have done. We want people to see this in our sexual purity. We also want them to hear it in his forgiveness. We want them to hear that though we have sinned—though they have sinned as well—we have one who can make us pure because he never sinned. His purity is ours and ours is his!

What do we tell people about sexual purity and sexual immorality?

We give them Jesus!

We are Jesus's people, who speak the truths of Jesus into the everyday stuff of life.

Speak the truths of Jesus for rightly ordering our budgets. Speak the truths of Jesus for finding a spouse. Speak the truths of Jesus for how we respond to our employers or employees. Speak the truths of Jesus for how we parent our children. Speak the truths of Jesus into everything.

Alisa needed the truths of Jesus—the gospel—spoken to her during our group time.

"Alisa," I said, "Jesus is the only man who will never let you down. Every other man will fail you, but he never will. God wants you to stop looking to your ex-husband, or any other man for that matter, to be for you what only Jesus can be for you. He wants Jesus to be at the center of your heart, your affections, and your hope. Jesus wants you to know that he loves you very much and wants to be your ultimate protector and provider."

"But how can I know for sure that he will take care of me?" she asked.

"Well, God loved you so much that he sent his only Son to die on the cross for your sins. While you were an enemy of God, God loved you enough to die for you so that you can be forgiven. You can be certain that he will provide for you. If he didn't hold back his only Son, you can be certain he will give you every other good gift that you need as well.

"And not only does he love you and want to provide for you," I continued, "but he also wants to set you free from the past. Jesus suffered for sin—your sin and the sin of others—so that you not only might be forgiven yourself, but also be able to forgive others and be healed of the wounds you've received through the sins done against you. God wants you to come to him through faith in Jesus for forgiveness and healing.

"We can eventually talk to your ex-husband if you'd like, but what is most important is that you meet Jesus, come to know his love for you, and be healed by him yourself. What is most important is that Jesus becomes the center of your life instead of your ex-husband or anything else. God alone can forgive, provide what you really need, and love you forever through what Jesus has done for you" (see John 3:16; Rom. 5:8; 8:32).

This was the beginning of many similar conversations with Alisa about Jesus.

This is what it looks like to speak the truths of Jesus into the everyday stuff of life. This is what it looks like for people to know Jesus in their everyday life, not just their afterlife.

This is gospel fluency.

Now, let's consider what it takes to become gospel fluent.

3

FLUENCY

Have you ever traveled to a place where the people didn't speak your native tongue? When I served as a youth pastor, we often took students on mission trips to places where the people spoke Spanish. To prepare everyone, we had our translator teach a crash course on the basics of Spanish. The team learned such phrases as "My name is . . ."; "I am hungry"; and "Where is the bathroom?" (*very important*). We also taught some basic cultural differences so that everyone on the team would be careful not to offend people unnecessarily. We spent months prior to our trips practicing Spanish with others who didn't know the language themselves (maybe not the best way to learn, since it was kind of like the blind leading the blind).

My wife, Jayne, who is definitely the more entertaining of the two of us, learned "Spanglish." In her goofiness, she had a little too much fun in the process. She put "el" at the front of words or "o" at the end while mixing in a little Spanish here and there: "Where-o is el bathroom-o?" "Me llamo is Jayne and I am very hungry-o"; or "My husband is very guapo and I want to kisso el jefe!" We were all very humored by her silliness.

Some of the team members tried speaking English really slowly, thinking that slowness would promote greater comprehension. When people still didn't understand, they spoke even slower, and louder, assuming the lack of understanding was due to speed or volume, not their deficiency in the language. Fortunately, the people we were serving expected this and were generally entertained by our foolishness. Our problem was that we knew just enough to sound as if we knew some Spanish, but we never knew enough to really have a conversation.

We too often do the same thing with our gospel training.

I'm thankful to say that more recently there has been a greater interest in receiving training in how to speak the gospel, both to one another in the church as well as to those outside it. However, our effectiveness, I'm afraid, has often been less than desired. Much of our training mirrors the approach and effectiveness of our language training for cross-cultural, short-term missions, and has led to similar experiences.

Gospelish

In Sunday school classes or church courses, we teach believers to sprinkle some gospel truths into their conversations. Or we give them a short presentation to share or a diagram to draw, which works really well if people are asking the questions the presentation or drawing addresses. However, in most cases, we and the people with whom we speak are like ships passing in the night because we are either giving answers to questions they are not asking or we are speaking a language none of us really understands that well.

So we go about "preaching" gospel snippets, thinking we're speaking the gospel to others, but what people hear is not good news. Oh, it might contain gospel elements, but they don't hear it as good news because they are not hearing the truths of Jesus applied to their lives and situations. What they get is just a set of phrases and propositions that don't make much sense to their context, culture, or language.

"Why does someone need to die for me? How does blood forgive sins? What is sin? Why does it really matter what I've done? How does a man who lived and died two thousand years ago help me?"

Much of our talk sounds a little like my wife's Spanglish.

I have found that most Christians don't really know why we need the gospel, what it is, why it is good news, and what it actually does—at least not enough to apply it to the everyday stuff of life. It's not that they *can't* know it well, but most aren't being equipped to become gospel-fluent people. Most believers have become gospel-snippet people, who speak gospel catchphrases. They're speaking gospelish, but not the actual gospel in a way people can hear and believe. They say: "Well, we preached the gospel, but they rejected it. People just have hard hearts and deaf ears."

Some of these believers get into debates and just speak louder, as our students did on mission trips, only creating greater objection to the gospel. Then they quote passages from the Bible about rejoicing in suffering for the sake of the gospel, when, in fact, people are just rejecting what they are saying because no good news is coming through.

Yes, I know the Bible teaches that the gospel is good news to those who are being saved and foolishness to those who are perishing, so it won't make sense to everyone. I know that we can't make people hear and believe. Some won't. It is God who saves, and it is God's Spirit who enables people to hear and understand the good news about Jesus Christ (1 Cor. 1:18; 2:14).

However, I'm not sure that we should just write ourselves an excuse when we preach what we believe is "good news." It may not be good news to our hearers if we don't take time to listen, understand, and then speak the gospel to the real brokenness and longing of their souls in a way that they can hear—a way that sounds like the good news of Jesus for them and their present situations.

We must do better at this.

It may be a laughing matter when we're talking about Spanglish. But it is no laughing matter when we're talking about the gospel of Jesus Christ and the lives of real, broken, lost people separated from God.

We have to become *gospel-fluent* people.

How Does Fluency Happen?

You gain fluency in a language when you move from merely translating an unfamiliar language into a familiar one to interpreting all of life through that new language. It happens when you can think, feel, and speak in a language. In a sense, the new language becomes the filter through which you perceive the world and help others perceive your world and theirs.

I spent the second semester of my junior year in college studying in Spain to fulfill my language requirement. Prior to leaving Michigan, I took a crash course in Spanish, learning some basic grammar and common phrases. It was similar to our mission teams' preparations. However, I was not going just for a week of serving with a group of English-speaking students. I was going to attend college in Spain, where the majority of my interactions would be in Spanish for more than four months.

I lived in a home where my host mom knew no English. Some of my professors spoke only Spanish, and the majority of the people in the town where I lived were unable to speak English at all. For the first month, I went to bed exhausted every night. Communication was tiresome. I had to listen very closely to people as they spoke Spanish (way too fast at first), process every word and phrase, translate into English, think about what I wanted to say in English, translate that back into Spanish in my head, and then speak it while trying to remember how to maneuver my mouth to say every word correctly. It was exhausting! So during this time, I learned to listen a lot and talk very little because talking was just too tiring.

After a few months of being immersed in constant Spanish for every moment—hearing it everywhere I went, reading it on every sign, listening to radio and television broadcasts in Spanish, and speaking it most of the day—I woke up one morning realizing I had been dreaming in Spanish. Something had changed. It became more normative for me to see something and describe it in my head with Spanish words and ideas.

Gradually, I stopped translating every word and phrase because I started thinking in Spanish. I even remember calling my parents in Michigan and, without thinking about it, talking to them in Spanish until they interrupted me and reminded me that they couldn't understand what I was saying.

I was becoming fluent.

Gospel Immersion

I believe such fluency is what God wants his people to experience with the gospel. He wants them to be able to translate the world around them and the world inside of them through the lens of the gospel—the truths of God revealed in the person and work of Jesus. Gospel-fluent people think, feel, and perceive everything in light of what has been accomplished in the person and work of Jesus Christ.

They see the world differently. They think differently. They feel differently.

When they are listening to people, they are thinking: "How is this in line with the truths of the gospel? What about Jesus and his work might be good news to this person today? How can I bring the hope of the gospel to bear on this life or situation so this person might experience salvation and Jesus will be glorified?"

When they see movies, they see the themes of the gospel, and they also notice which themes represent a false gospel. They begin to evaluate the storylines of their surrounding culture in light of the story of God's redemptive purposes in Christ Jesus, and they learn to perceive where God might already be at work around them, preparing the soil of a community and individual hearts for the seeds of the gospel to be sown.

Most significantly, those who are growing in gospel fluency are experiencing ongoing transformation themselves.

They are experiencing ongoing change as the truths of the gospel are brought to bear on their thoughts, beliefs, emotions, and actions, transforming them into greater Christlikeness every day.

They are growing up into Christ in every way because they are learning to hear and speak the truths of Jesus Christ into everything.

They are becoming gospel fluent.

The gospel is becoming their native tongue because it was through the gospel that they were born again. It is by the gospel that they find themselves growing up into Christ. And they are convinced that the gospel will keep them to the end and perfect them into the true image of Christ.

To use theological language, the gospel is becoming their native tongue because it brought about their regeneration, justification, and adoption; it is bringing about their sanctification;

and it will bring about their eventual glorification. It is the beginning, the middle, and the end of their new life in Christ.

The gospel is everything to them.

But gospel fluency does not come about only in a classroom or during Sunday morning gatherings. In other words, people don't become fluent through classes or by passively listening to preaching—or even by reading a book.

They become fluent through immersion in a gospel-speaking culture.

You *do* need to receive some formal training in the basics of the gospel, just as learning a language requires knowing the basics of grammar, vocabulary, and sentence structure. That is why I dedicate the next section of this book, "The Gospel," to laying out the basic principles of the gospel. You need to know the basics of the gospel in order to become fluent in the gospel.

However, formal training alone does not make one fluent. You become fluent through immersion in a gospel-speaking community and through ongoing practice. You have to know it, regularly hear it, and practice proclaiming it. That is why the final three sections are entitled "The Gospel in Me," "The Gospel with Us," and "The Gospel to Others."

Gospel fluency begins in you, gets worked out within community, and is expressed to a world that needs to hear about Jesus.

Your ongoing development in the gospel best occurs through involvement in a gospel-proclaiming church—a people who gather regularly to hear the good news of Jesus spoken. Please, if you want to grow in gospel fluency, gather with a church that regularly preaches the good news of Jesus Christ. I am also convinced that people need to participate throughout the week in a gospel community on mission or in a missional community,[1] where the members consistently bring the gospel to bear on one

---

1. For more on missional community, read my other book, *Saturate: Being Disciples of Jesus in the Everyday Stuff of Life* (Wheaton, IL: Crossway, 2015), or go to saturatetheworld.com.

another's lives and on the lives of those who don't yet believe in Jesus.

Whenever I start a new missional community, I begin by asking people to share their stories. I encourage people to listen with "gospel ears" for what people believe has saved them and is saving them. I also encourage them to listen for who or what is the hero of each story.[2] And I spend several weeks laying down a gospel foundation, making sure people understand what the gospel is, what it does, and how to apply the truths of Jesus to the everyday stuff of life. Much like my crash course in Spanish during college, I believe we have to establish people in the basics of the gospel if they are ever going to become fluent in speaking the gospel.

Then I encourage the group members never to settle for having a time together where they don't listen well and look for opportunities to speak the truths of Jesus into the conversations they are having or the situations they are facing. It's not a good night of Christian community if Christ isn't present in our thoughts and conversations. We need to—*we get to*—talk about Jesus whenever we come together. He's the whole reason we exist and function in this world.

Language fluency requires immersion into a community of people who speak the language constantly. Gospel fluency requires immersion into a community of people so saturated with the gospel of Jesus Christ that they just can't stop speaking the truths of Jesus wherever they go and in whatever situations they find themselves.

Always Talking about Jesus

Several years ago, a young woman spent the summer with us to fulfill her college requirement for an internship. At the end of the summer, our leadership team threw her a going-away party. During the party, we provided some space for her to reflect on

---

2. There is more on this in chapter 12, "The Hero of Our Story."

her time with us. One of our leaders specifically asked her what was different from what she had expected.

She paused for a moment and then said: "Well, this might sound a little strange, but the thing that most surprised me was how much you all talk about Jesus. I mean, I know we believe in Jesus and this is supposed to be all about Jesus, but you guys talk about him all the time. Every day, every meeting, every situation—you're always talking about Jesus!

"At first, I just thought you were strange. Then, I started to think maybe something was wrong with me—that I didn't really know and love Jesus. The church I came from talks about Jesus here and there—especially when we have an evangelistic Sunday. However, most of the teaching is about us—about what we should do and how we need to change. We might hear three key ideas on how to better manage our time or five principles for engaging in serving. But we don't hear Jesus preached every week through every Bible text, and we certainly don't talk about Jesus whenever we get together.

"To be honest, while I was with you all, I began to wonder if I was even saved. And, well, I'm not sure how to say this, but I think I finally came to really know and love Jesus this summer with you. It was just impossible to get away from hearing how great Jesus is with you all!"

We were so encouraged to hear this!

Gospel fluency is developed by being immersed into a Jesus-saturated community. A Jesus-saturated community knows and speaks the gospel every day into everything, so that all parts of our lives grow up into Christ and are eventually fully transformed by and submitted to Jesus Christ, who is everything for us (Eph. 1:22–23; 4:15; Col. 1:15–20).

That is how gospel fluency happens, but let's first start with what the gospel is.

What is the gospel?

PART 2

THE GOSPEL

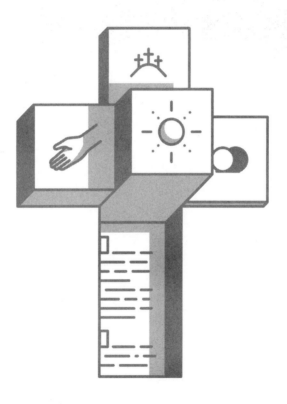

4

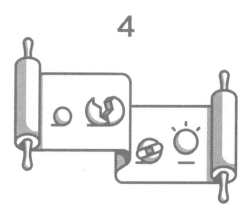

THE TRUE STORY

When learning a new language, you study vocabulary (words and their meanings), grammar (how to structure the words into meaningful sentences), and culture (what the words actually mean in context). When you're a child, you learn a language orally in the culture where you are brought up, and that culture plays a very significant role in your understanding and speaking of the language. In fact, some of the dictionary definitions of words do not always line up with the cultural meanings of those words because the cultural context has given them new meanings.

For instance, one dictionary defines a cat as "a small domesticated carnivorous mammal with soft fur, a short snout, and retractile claws. It is widely kept as a pet or for catching mice, and many breeds have been developed."[1] I, on the other hand, grew up believing that cats were actually little demons looking to take the lives of small children if they could, while also giving me significant breathing problems due to my allergic reaction to them—which I, of course, understood as God's way of protecting me from the evil spirits!

That's a little extreme, I know, but you get the point.

Then, through hanging out with some of my African American friends, I learned that a cat is actually an adult male who is highly skilled in a particular craft—such as music, the spoken word, sports, or preaching. "Listen to that cat! He's dope!" (not referring to something you smoke, of course).

So culture shapes language.

Likewise, language shapes culture. Do you want to change a culture? Change or redefine the language. You change or redefine language through story. If you want a new or redefined language, tell a new story.

Story gives meaning to language. Every word we know has meaning because of the story in which that word was defined.

If I say "Aslan," some of you think of a Christlike lion king. And when you read *The Lion King*, some of you think of Simba and start singing, "I just can't wait to be king!" Some of you don't know what I'm talking about because you've never read *The Lion, the Witch and the Wardrobe* by C. S. Lewis or viewed Disney's animated movie about a cowardly young lion growing up to be the courageous king of the jungle. And it's very possible that after reading these sentences together, some of you are now looking for parallels or divergent themes as you compare both stories.

The stories of our lives are especially powerful in shaping

---

1. Angus Stevenson, ed., *Oxford Dictionary of English*, 3rd ed. (Oxford: Oxford University Press, 2010), 272.

how we understand and interpret language. For some, the word *father* is a wonderful term that conjures up all kinds of tender emotions—love, care, and feelings of provision and protection. When others hear the word *father*, they feel abandonment, emotional disengagement, rejection, and fear.

Culture shapes language. Language shapes culture. And stories have the power to redefine or create new language. Our words have meaning because of the stories in which they are used. And we understand our words from the story *we* find ourselves in.

So how do we become a gospel-centered culture full of gospel-fluent people? We need gospel language that is correctly shaped by the gospel story.

All of us are living our lives under a dominant story. We perceive the world and human interactions through the stories we know and believe. For most of us, that is our story of origin, our family story. This is a much smaller story inside the larger one, and often it leads us to wrong perceptions of God, ourselves, others, and the world around us. In some cases, we believe outright lies.

But there is a true story. It's the story of God found in the Bible. It's the story that redeems, heals, and completes our personal stories—the smaller stories within the true story.

We will talk about the makeup of the gospel (like vocabulary) and how it has meaning for our lives (like grammar), but we first need to get the overarching story because it is the true story that informs the meaning of the gospel.

Other authors have dedicated entire books[2] to the true story, and there are some helpful tools[3] that can guide a group

---

2. See Craig Bartholomew and Michael Goheen, *The Drama of Scripture: Finding Our Place in the Biblical Story* (Grand Rapids, MI: Baker Academic, 2014); Bartholomew and Goheen, *The True Story of the Whole World: Finding Your Place in the Biblical Drama* (Grand Rapids, MI: Faith Alive, 2009); Justin Buzzard, *The Big Story: How the Bible Makes Sense Out of Life* (Chicago: Moody, 2013).

3. See *The Story-Formed Way*, https://saturatetheworld.com/story-formed-way/; *The Story of God*, https://saturatetheworld.com/story-of-god; and *The Story of God for Kids*, https://saturatetheworld.com/story-of-god-for-kids.

through the story together, but for the purposes of this book, I am going to walk through a summary narrative of the true story using four key movements: Creation, Fall, Redemption, and New Creation.

Creation

"In the beginning God . . ." (Gen. 1:1).

That is how the story begins—with God.

God eternally existed in community—God the Father, God the Son, and God the Holy Spirit—one God in three persons, existing in perfect unity. Nothing else existed.

In the beginning, God created by his word. He created the heavens and the earth out of nothing. He spoke and it all came into being.

God's word brought about God's work.

God designed a beautiful place full of everything necessary for life where humans could live.[4] Then he created man and woman in his image, after his likeness. The invisible God created humans to be a visible display—a picture—of what he is like. After creating, God said that it was *very good*, then rested from the work of creating. That was essentially God's way of saying: "I did great work! I am satisfied with what I have done. This is righteous." God wanted the man and the woman to know that he declared them good—he declared them righteous.

God's word is powerful and true. His work is very good. Rest in it.

Why is this so important?

Well, if everything came into existence through the word of God, and if everything that comes into existence through God's word is good, then God's word and work are to be completely trusted and depended upon. We have our very existence

---

4. This part of the story is found in Genesis 1–2.

through his word and work. Therefore, our identity, purpose, and truth are all to be found in God's word and God's work.

Not just in the beginning—always.

The questions "Who am I?" and "Why am I here?" are not meant to be answered outside of what God says and what God does.

Before we go any further, ask yourself: "Who or what do I look to—trust in, depend upon—for my worth?"

God also created work for the man to do by creating a garden for him to care for. He commanded the man, saying, "You may surely eat of every tree of the garden, but of the tree of the knowledge of good and evil you shall not eat, for in the day that you eat of it you shall surely die" (Gen. 2:16–17). God called the man to look to him, not creation and not his own work, for his identity. He called the man to look to him for purpose and truth. Eating of that tree would be essentially turning to another source for identity, purpose, and truth.

God called the man to trust him and obey him: "Believe who I say you are. Trust in what I've done to make you who you are. And as a result, do what I command."

At this point in the story, the man was still alone. No suitable helper for him was around yet. No friend, partner, or mate—just the animals. And God said that it was *not* good that the man was alone. (This is a good reminder that a dog is not man's best friend.)

So God made a helper fit for the man. He put the man to sleep and took a rib out of his body. The first surgery in the history of the world led to the first woman, made from a man. When the man woke up from his slumber, he saw the beauty in front of him and exclaimed, "This at last is bone of my bones and flesh of my flesh; she shall be called Woman, because she was taken out of Man" (Gen. 2:23).

The woman was made from man. And together, they were a

picture of the unity and community of God. God commanded them to "be fruitful and multiply and fill the earth and subdue it, and have dominion over [it]" (Gen. 1:28). They were called to submit to God, rule over the earth on behalf of God, and fill it with more image bearers who would do the same.

A mandate to love, work, and rule in such a way as to show all of creation what God is like.

A good and beautiful garden.

A man and woman living in harmonious and pure love, naked and unashamed, daily enjoying each other, working and ruling over creation, and interacting with God in their midst.

It was all very good! But that was about to change.

Fall

They didn't believe. They didn't trust God's word and work.

The problem was unbelief. The action was sin. The result was death.

The Serpent, the Devil, convinced the woman that God's word was a lie and his work was not good: "God knows you aren't as good as you could be. He knows that if you just take matters into your own hands, you will be much better. You can be like God if you just eat the fruit he told you not to eat."[5]

She believed the lie and ate the fruit, then she gave some to her husband, and he ate too.

God had told them they were very good—they were made in his image, after his likeness. But they didn't believe him. Instead, they believed the Devil, the master of lies. God had told them they would surely die if they ate the fruit. But they didn't believe him. Instead, they believed the lie of the Devil, that they wouldn't die. As a result of their rebellion, sin entered the world and brought about death and destruction.

---

5. This part of the story is found in Genesis 3.

When I shared Romans 6:23 with our missional community recently, one of the new believers in the group asked, "If the wages of sin is death, and if God promised Adam and Eve they would surely die if they ate of the tree, why didn't they die?"

"Well, they did die," I responded.

"But why didn't they die immediately?" she retorted.

It seemed she understood the severity of their rebellion and wondered why God didn't just strike them down then and there.

I responded: "Well, the death God was referring to wasn't just a physical one. It was spiritual, relational, and physical. Besides, if he had destroyed them then and there, it would have been the end of humanity. God didn't want to destroy humanity. He loved them and wanted to save them. He wanted to rescue them from the consequences of their sin."

Then I went on to explain what I meant by spiritual, relational, and physical death.

Adam and Eve rebelled against God by looking elsewhere for identity, purpose, and truth. They looked away from the giver and sustainer of life to the one who is committed to taking and destroying life instead.[6] This led to a *spiritual* death, or brokenness in their relationship with God. They turned from submitting to and believing in God to trusting in and submitting to Satan.

In that moment, Adam and Eve surrendered their God-given authority over the world to Satan. They were meant to rule the world on behalf of God. But they gave that authority to the Devil, who became known as "the god of this world" (2 Cor. 4:4; cf. John 12:31).

We see the results of this spiritual death immediately in the shame they felt, which led to a desire to cover themselves with clothing they made out of fig leaves. And they immediately

---

6. Jesus said in John 10:10: "The thief [the Devil] comes to steal and kill and destroy. I came that they may have life and have it abundantly."

hid themselves from God when they heard him coming near. If they had trusted in God's word and work, they would have had no need to hide or cover up because they would not have been guilty or felt any shame. They would have had no reason to be afraid.

The second death was *relational* in nature. Our relationship with God affects every other relationship. Before their sinful rebellion, Adam and Eve were perfectly united, naked and unashamed in each other's presence. However, after they sinned, they turned on each other and blamed each other. They were looking for someone to pay for what they had done. This is called atonement—payment for sin. However, neither could pay for the other because both had sinned. Only an innocent one could do that.

Both were guilty. Both needed to pay for their own sin.

When we sin, we feel shame, and then we look to blame someone. Someone has to pay. Everyone intuitively knows and feels this. Humans feel this because we are image bearers of God. We reflect God's perfect, loving justice. We long for things to be made right.

Some of us blame others for sin, and hate or despise them because we want them to pay for what has been done. Some of us blame ourselves and try to pay for our sin through self-loathing, self-hurting, religion, or good works. Adam and Eve did both.

We are to blame for our sin. We are guilty, and because we are, we need someone else to pay for our sin.

Adam and Eve had that need too.

That leads to the third kind of death, *physical* death.

God covered the man and woman with the skins of an animal (Gen. 3:21). An innocent animal died so their shame could be covered. This is the first sacrifice for sins that we see in the story. Eventually, an innocent human would have to willingly die to atone for our sin, remove our guilt, and cover our shame.

Until then, sacrifices for sin would be made, but they would never be enough to truly forgive sin or make people new. People would continue to sin, and sin would continue to destroy. People would be born, be hurt, and die. This pattern continued from generation to generation.

We see this in the very next story in the Bible, as the same relational discord that afflicted Adam and Eve was passed on to their children.[7] Cain killed Abel out of jealousy for his brother's acceptable offering to God. Cain, like his parents, didn't want to heed God's word for acceptance. He put his hope in his own work instead. But his work fell short. And again, someone else suffered for sin.

Sin produces death. Enemies kill one another. So do jealous brothers. Eventually, everyone dies.

And this physical death doesn't just affect humanity. All of creation is affected as humanity's sin wreaks havoc on our world. We see the physical effects of sin producing death and destruction everywhere on the planet as we continue to kill it with our selfishness and greed.

The wages of sin *is* death—spiritual, relational, and physical.

Sinful rebellion produces brokenness, suffering, and death.

This is because rebellion against God is rebellion against the giver of life. And this rebellion began and continues to go on because of unbelief in the truthfulness of God's word and the sufficiency of his work.

Redemption

Thankfully, the story doesn't end with destruction and death. Even as the man and woman were being informed about the curse of sin and its effects on their lives and relationships, God

---

7. This part of the story is found in Genesis 4.

also promised to put an end to the Serpent and the rebellion he had started. Through Eve's offspring, Satan would eventually be crushed (Gen. 3:15).

God would have the final word. He would save us from our sin. He would rescue us from Satan. He would put death to death.

His word is true and his work is sufficient.

As the story continued, things went from bad to worse. But God never let things get as bad as they could. He regularly put an end to the progression of evil to prevent humanity from completely wiping itself out. The flood is one of the greatest examples of this.[8] A time came when every intention of the human heart was evil all the time. That was really bad! God was sad he had created man. However, he still saved them. He did it through a great flood. He cleansed the earth of all the evil and chose one man through whom humanity would get another chance.

Noah was that man. He found favor in the eyes of God, which means God showed grace toward him. After the flood subsided and Noah and his family left the ark, God reminded him of the mandate: "Be fruitful and multiply and fill the earth" (Gen. 9:1). God also informed Noah that the life source of humanity is in the blood, so blood must be shed when life is taken, since man is made in the image of God (vv. 4–6). This set in place the concept that blood needs to be shed for the forgiveness of our sins. Since all sin is rebellion against God, blood—the source of life, including our life—must be given as payment (Lev. 17:11; Heb. 9:22).

Noah's family did multiply. And things began to get bad again. Sin was still present, and people continued to rebel against God.

Eventually, God called a man named Abram to be the one

---

8. This part of the story is found in Genesis 6–8.

through whom he would start a family for his purposes on the earth.[9] He promised Abram that he would make of him a great nation, that he would bless him, and that he would make his name great, so that through him all the people groups on the earth would be blessed.

Abram and Sarai, his wife, had no children at the time and both were too old to conceive. Yet God promised. And Abram believed God's word and trusted in God's work, and God counted it to him as righteousness. God changed his name to Abraham, meaning "father of many nations." This new name represented the new work God would do through Abraham.

God gave Abraham and his wife a son named Isaac, who became the father of Jacob, who became the father of twelve sons, through whom were founded the twelve tribes of Israel. One of those tribes was Judah, through whom the promised offspring, Jesus, eventually would come into the world.

God rescued Jacob's family, who become the nation of Israel, from famine through the provision of Egypt.[10] It was in that place that they grew in number. It was also there that they became slaves to Pharaoh. God sent Moses to confront Pharaoh and demand that he let God's people go. Pharaoh refused, despite the many plagues God brought upon the land. Then God took Pharaoh's firstborn son and all the other firstborn sons of Egypt. Pharaoh finally relented and God's people were released.[11]

They were redeemed from slavery to go to the land God had promised them. This land was to resemble a garden like the first. It would be a land of plenty where God's people could rest in him and his provision, where God would be present with the people, and where his image could once again be expressed.

Abraham's family was redeemed to rest. They were called to God to display and declare his goodness.

---

9. This part of the story is found in Genesis 12–18, 21.

10. To see how God accomplished this through Joseph, read Genesis 37–50.

11. This part of the story is found in Exodus 1–14.

Redemption became the running theme of the story as God continued to call his people to trust him by reminding them of what he had done for them and to obey him in light of their faith in him. Over and over, they forgot and failed to trust and obey. And over and over again, God rescued them from their slavery. Often the slavery was physical in nature, but it always reflected the spiritual slavery to sin to which they had submitted themselves.

God chose, called, and created Israel. He blessed them to be a blessing to the nations. God set them apart as his holy people. They were called to trust and obey God and, in so doing, to be a visible display of what God is like to the nations.

Israel was to be to God as a son who displays what his father is like.

But Israel failed. God's plan, however, did not. He would still fulfill his word. Through the offspring, the world would be blessed. Another son—the true Son of God—would accomplish it.

Jesus is that Son.

Jesus came as the true and better Adam, the true and better Abraham, and the true and better Israel. God's full and final redemption to rescue us from slavery to sin and Satan came in the form of a baby.

He is God's redemption plan. He always was—even before the creation of the world.

He was conceived by the Holy Spirit and born of the virgin Mary, yet he was without sin. He lived the life we were created to live, perfectly trusting in and submitting to God the Father. He overcame Satan's temptation, and served and ministered as the King of kings, who came not to be served but to serve by laying down his life in our place. He died as our atoning sacrifice, shedding his blood on the cross for our sin, removing our guilt, and covering our shame. He was buried and rose again on the third day, triumphant over Satan, sin, and death as the firstfruits of a new creation.

This leads to the last part of the story.

New Creation

Jesus was raised with a glorified body. He took on our sin at the cross, where he paid for it with his blood and destroyed its power. He overcame death and was given new life. And in his glorified, sinless body that can no longer be taken down by Satan, sin, or death, he has been given all authority in heaven and earth.

Jesus is the new and better Adam over a new and better creation.

And through his body, lifeless in the tomb, God brought forth another woman—the second woman to be brought forth from a man's body.

God brought forth the church.

The church is Jesus's bride. We are God's new-creation people (2 Cor. 5:17). All those who believe in Jesus's life, death, and resurrection go from having Adam as their authority and life source to having Jesus as the new Adam. Adam sinned, and everyone born since then was born into sin as a result.

Everyone except Jesus.

Conceived by the Holy Spirit of God, he was born without sin and is the very righteousness of God. When we are born again by the Spirit, we are brought under Jesus as our new Adam—our new life source and our new authority (head). Thus, he is the beginning of a new creation.

We are Jesus's bride (John 3:29; Eph. 5:22–33; Rev. 19:7; 21:2, 9), the church, and God's children, the family of God (Mark 3:33–35; John 1:12–13; Rom. 8:14–17; Eph. 1:3–6).

We have been transferred from the kingdom of darkness, with Satan as lord, to the kingdom of light, with Jesus as Lord

(Col. 1:13–14). We have been changed from being spiritually dead in our sins to being alive in Christ, able to live new lives because of him (Eph. 2:1–10). We went from being sinners to saints, from enemies of God to dearly loved children of God, and from powerless to overcome sin to mightily empowered by the Spirit to defeat sin.

Jesus was given all authority in heaven and earth, and all who are his share that authority in order to fulfill his mission. With this authority, Jesus commands us to make disciples of all nations, establish them in their new identity[12] in Christ, and teach them to obey Jesus's commands. Just as Adam and Eve were called to be fruitful, multiply, and fill the earth and subdue it, we are commissioned by and with Jesus to make disciples.[13] What is called the Great Commission is really the new creation mandate under Jesus as our head.

Everything has changed. Our identity and our purpose, as well as our understanding of the truths of God, have completely changed.

We also have a future hope. The new creation is not just personal but cosmic.

God will bring about a new heaven and new earth, which we will get to live in and enjoy forever. The true image of God, Jesus, will light up that world with his glory, and we also, with renewed resurrection bodies, will reflect God as redeemed, re-created, and resurrected image bearers, transformed by the glory of Christ.

We will forever dwell in the gardenlike city, where there will be no suffering or pain, sin or sorrow, brokenness or despair, sickness or death. All of God's enemies will have been captured and crushed, and all that is wrong will have been made right.[14]

---

12. That is what happens in our baptism. Remember, Jesus told his disciples to baptize into *the name of* the triune God (see Matt. 28:19).

13. He said he would be with us always, to the end of the age (Matt. 28:20).

14. This part of the story is found in Revelation 21–22.

Those of us who know and love Jesus long for that day.

However, we also let that future reality inform our present behavior. We let what we know about it inform what we do about the brokenness we see around us every day. Because we are already new creations in Christ, we invite the future hope into our present lives through the Holy Spirit, who raised Jesus from the dead. We, as his people, become a foretaste of the future, pointing forward to a better day by giving people a taste of it now.

Certainly we can't provide the full taste—only Jesus can, and will in the end. But he is in us and at work through us to show the world what God is like. Through our lives, Jesus is saying, "Taste and see that the Lord is good!" The new creation has already begun in Jesus and has begun in us, and one day he will bring it to full completion.

Until then, we live as the redeemed people of God, becoming more and more like Jesus every day so that more and more people come to him through our visible and verbal testimony.

This is our story.

This is *the* story.

This is the true and better story that can redeem and make new every other story.

You want to change a culture? Give them a new story. Language will follow.

5

POWER FOR SALVATION

When people say they are *saved*, what do they mean?

Suppose someone says, "I was saved when I was ten." Saved from what? I have to be honest and say that I am very concerned that most people who grew up in the church don't actually know what they mean when they say things like this. At the least, they have a very minimalist view of salvation: "I've been saved from going to hell when I die because I prayed a prayer I was instructed to pray."

This was my view for many years. I had no idea that God's salvation wasn't dependent upon my prayer and is so powerful and all-encompassing that it deals with more than just our afterlife (though it does deal with that).

We were powerless to save ourselves. We were dead in our sins, enemies of God, and, by nature, children of wrath. We were helpless and hopeless, slaves to sin and Satan. We needed to be saved from the power of Satan, sin, and death. We also needed to be saved from the wrath of God against sin.

I want to be very clear. We do not save ourselves. We cannot save ourselves. We do nothing in terms of our salvation. God does everything.

When we talk about the gospel, we are not just talking about a doctrine we write down and quote. We are talking about the very real, dynamic power of God to create, redeem, and save. The power I'm talking about brought the world into existence. It's the same power that breathed life into dust and formed a man. This power struck down the Egyptians and parted the Red Sea so that all of Israel could pass through on dry ground. The power we proclaim in the gospel is the same power that was visible on top of Mount Sinai, ablaze with fire; that was exerted to conquer Israel's enemies; and that helped David defeat Goliath with one stone.

The power of the gospel is the power that enabled Jesus to overcome temptation, preach with authority, cast out demons, heal the sick, raise the dead, and rise from the dead himself.

The gospel is not just dogma, though it is doctrine we believe. It's not just history, though it is historical. It's not just past, though it happened. The gospel is the power of God made available to us through the Son of God, who gave his life for us. He is alive and at work in those who believe by his Spirit. And that power was exerted, is presently available, and will keep us safe until the end.

The gospel is the *power* of God for salvation for our entire lives.

In my first book, *Saturate*, I wrote about God's power to save us—past, present, and future. We *have been* saved from the penalty of sin; we *are being* saved from the power of sin; and we *will be* saved from the presence of sin. In this chapter, I want to delve into God's power to save in greater detail.

Think of this chapter as a vocabulary lesson. To become fluent in any language, you must develop your vocabulary. So let's delve into the aspects of the gospel that are expressed in the person and work of Jesus.

Belief in the gospel is not a one-time decision or a conviction that we need salvation only for our past lives and future afterlives. Belief in the gospel is an ongoing expression of our ongoing need for Jesus. Standing firm in it means we continue to put our faith in him for our past, our present, and our future.

Paul addressed a very broken church in his first letter to the believers in Corinth. Their lives were a visible display of their unbelief in God and the gospel. According to Paul, they had come to believe the gospel, but then they began living in a way that showed they were not standing firm in the truths of the gospel. So he clarified the basics of the gospel in 1 Corinthians 15:1–6:

> Now I would remind you, brothers, of the gospel I preached to you, which you received, *in which you stand*, and by which *you are being saved*, if you hold fast to the word I preached to you—unless you believed in vain. For I delivered to you as of first importance what I also received: that *Christ died for our sins* in accordance with the Scriptures, that *he was buried*, that *he was raised on the third day* in accordance with the Scriptures, and that *he appeared* to Cephas, then to the twelve. Then he appeared to more than five hundred brothers at one time, most of whom are still alive, though some have fallen asleep.

The gospel is the power of God for salvation to all who *believe* (Rom. 1:16).

What do we believe? What are we putting our faith in?

Jesus's Life

Let's start with the life of Jesus. "Wait a minute," you might be thinking. "Paul starts with his death. Isn't the gospel about Jesus's death?"

Well, there is no death if there is no life. Paul assumes this in saying "Christ died."

Too many people forget the life of Christ when they talk about the cross of Christ. But if we don't have the perfect life of Jesus, we can have no confidence in the death of Jesus. The righteousness revealed in the gospel (Rom. 1:17) requires the perfect obedience of Jesus.

Jesus's life represents both the righteousness of God in human form and the perfect fulfillment of the standard of righteousness on behalf of humanity. If you want to know what the righteousness of God looks like, you look at Jesus's life, and if you want to be declared righteous by God, you need to have faith in how Jesus lived on your behalf, not just in how he died.

Because of sin, we were all powerless to live righteous lives that would be acceptable to God. Even our best attempts fell woefully short.

Remember our story.

In prideful arrogance and selfish ambition, Adam and Eve disobeyed God. They had been made in God's image, created in God's likeness, but they sinned and fell short of his glory. They didn't trust and obey God, and as a result, they failed to display the truth about what God is like in their thoughts, motives, and actions. The Bible calls this sin. All humans since Adam have been born into sin and prove themselves to be sinners as well. "All have sinned and fall short of the glory of God" (Rom. 3:23). Not one of us trusts and obeys God, and as a result, we have all failed to display the truth about what God is like in our thoughts, motives, and actions.

We all needed a new human to give birth to a new humanity—

a perfect man who is also the true image of God, fully display-ing what God is like by living a fully submitted and obedient life before God. Jesus is that man. "He is the image of the invisible God, the firstborn of all creation" (Col. 1:15).

It wasn't enough for him to just show up on earth and die for our sins. He had to live the life we don't live in order for him to be for us the righteousness of God we aren't—the life that God rightly demands that we live. You see, God doesn't just want us to have a zero balance in our sin account. He expects us to have a full and complete balance in our righteousness ac-count. That's the standard. His expectation for the human life is his glory—living in such a way as to display and declare what he is really like in everything we feel, think, and do.

So Jesus was conceived by the Holy Spirit of God and was born of the virgin Mary, but without sin. The eternal Son of God took on flesh and dwelt among sinful humanity. He lived for thirty years in obscurity and humility. God was in the neigh-borhood, but almost nobody, except some angels and smelly shepherds, recognized him. Paul describes this humility in Phi-lippians 2:6–8: "Though he was in the form of God, [he] did not count equality with God a thing to be grasped, but emptied him-self, by taking the form of a servant, being born in the likeness of men. And being found in human form, he humbled himself by becoming obedient to the point of death, even death on a cross."

Adam, full of pride, sought equality with God. Jesus, full of humility, even though he was in nature God, emptied himself and did not seek to grasp hold of equality, but instead became a servant. Jesus, the Son of God, did not come to be served but to serve and give up his life as a ransom for many (Matt. 20:28; Mark 10:45). And he lived the only perfectly righteous human life ever. He is God's righteousness. He gave himself for us to be our righteousness before God.

Then, before he began his ministry of proclaiming and

displaying the good news of God's kingdom, he entered the waters of baptism for the repentance of sin to fulfill all righteousness (Matt. 3:13–17; Mark 1:9–11; Luke 3:21–22).

Why did he need to do this? He never sinned. He had no need to repent!

Jesus was not baptized because he had sinned. He did it to identify with sinners—those who need to turn to God for forgiveness. In his righteousness, he identified with our sinfulness. He did not come for the righteous; he came for sinners (Mark 2:17). In his baptism, Jesus was saying: "I will identify with you so that you can identify with me. I will take on your sin so you can take on my righteousness." As he came out of the waters of baptism, the Spirit descended upon him and God the Father spoke over him, saying, "You are my beloved Son; with you I am well pleased" (Mark 1:11).

Following this, the Spirit led him into the wilderness to be tempted by the Devil. Unlike Adam and Eve, Jesus overcame. He didn't give in to the temptation. He is our righteousness and our overcomer—victorious over Satan's schemes. After that, he could proclaim the good news (gospel) that the kingdom of God was present because an image bearer of God—*the true image of God*—was taking back authority from Satan.

The true and better ruler had come and the kingdom of God was being expressed and experienced in and with Jesus. The good news has a King and a kingdom. This is why he is called Jesus Christ. Christ is not his last name. It is his title: Jesus the Christ. *Christ* is a transliteration of the Greek word for the King who is anointed by God to deliver his people from sin and Satan. Jesus has this power to rescue us out of darkness and bring us into his kingdom of light. His entire ministry is about the proclamation and demonstration of the kingdom of God—life as it should be under God's rule and reign as opposed to slavery under Satan's.

This is a very important part of the gospel. It is the gospel of the kingdom of God.

We need more than the humble life of Christ. We also need the victorious rule and ministry of Christ to overcome Satan's schemes, bring healing and restoration to the brokenness that sin produces, and provide reconciliation between God and man.

Jesus's Death

Eventually, Jesus was betrayed, arrested, wrongly accused, and crucified. The perfect Son of God, the righteousness of God, the one who knew no sin, became sin at the cross so that we might become the righteousness of God in him (2 Cor. 5:21).

We needed a perfect substitute—one without sin, fully pleasing to God—who would die in our place. The Bible says, "For the wages of sin is death, but the free gift of God is eternal life in Christ Jesus our Lord" (Rom. 6:23). Our sin, our rebellion, every way in which we fall short of the glory of God, was put on Jesus at the cross. His perfect life was exchanged for our life of sin.

At the cross, Jesus atoned for our sins—he paid the debt we couldn't pay and suffered the death we should have experienced. At the cross, the wrath of God for sin was completely satisfied. Jesus is the propitiation for our sins (Rom. 3:25; Heb. 2:17; 1 John 2:2; 4:10). This means that God's anger against our sin was satisfied by Jesus's death for sin. And God's love for his own Son was poured out for sinners (John 17:23, 26).

When Jesus went to the cross, he was wounded for our transgressions, so that by his wounds we might be healed (Isa. 53:5). Jesus died to forgive us of our sins, to cleanse us from all unrighteousness, and to heal us from all the pain and brokenness that sin produces. Because of the cross, we become reconciled to God. We go from being God's enemies—who, because of our sinful nature, were objects of wrath—to dearly loved children of God (Rom. 5:8; 8:14–17; Eph. 1:3–5; 2:1–6).

And Jesus died. He was *really* dead. He didn't just go to sleep. He didn't fall into a coma. He died and was buried in a tomb.

Jesus died for our sins. He took our sins on himself—on his real physical, human body—and then died for them. Our sins were buried with Jesus. They were not just removed and put in another place. They were destroyed by his death.

Death is terminal. Our sins were terminated.

If your faith is in Jesus, your sins, past, present, and future, were terminated through Jesus's death.

And he didn't die just to remove our sins from us, but also to destroy the power of sin over us. Paul says: "There is therefore now no condemnation for those who are in Christ Jesus. For the law of the Spirit of life has set you free in Christ Jesus from the law of sin and death. For God has done what the law, weakened by the flesh, could not do. By sending his own Son in the likeness of sinful flesh and for sin, he condemned sin in the flesh" (Rom. 8:1–3).

He condemned sin, destroying its power.

Jesus's Resurrection

And how do we know Jesus destroyed the power of sin and death?

He rose again from the dead.

Jesus put death to death. He was raised on the third day and appeared to more than five hundred people. He was raised with a glorified body, one without sin. This was a body for the new creation.

Paul calls Jesus the firstfruits of what will ultimately be true for all of us who are in Christ, who have faith in him (1 Cor. 15:20–23). Eventually, we will each be given glorified, resurrected bodies that are without sin, so that we may live in a new heaven and new earth forever.

Until that day, we have the presence of the resurrected Jesus in our weak and frail bodies to enable us to live a new life now. We have his Spirit.

The gospel doesn't just bring about forgiveness of sins and save us from hell. The gospel of Jesus Christ empowers us to live a whole new life today by the same Spirit who raised Jesus from the dead.

There's no greater power than that!

In fact, after Jesus rose from the dead, he ascended to the right hand of God the Father, where he is now making intercession on our behalf. He is continually praying for us, willing to empower us by his Spirit in us, and speaking a better word over us than Satan, sin, or our past experiences speak. We trust in the word of Jesus and the work of Jesus before God on our behalf. We are not like Adam and Eve, who put their trust in another word and another work. We look to and put our faith in the word of God and the work of God for our righteousness.

After Jesus's resurrection and ascension, God sent his Spirit to wake us up from spiritual death, convict us of our sin, make the truths of the gospel clear to our hearts, grant us repentance and faith, and bring about new life as a result. By his Spirit, we are born again from the dead, spiritually speaking (John 3:5–8, 14–16; Eph. 2:1). We become new creations in Christ (2 Cor. 5:17). Each of us has a new nature, a new identity, and a new purpose. And the Spirit in those who believe is a sign of all of this. The Spirit is also the means by which we have the power to live entirely new and different lives. He is the sign that we are forgiven and cleansed, changed and made new, chosen and adopted by God—he wants us, he chose us, he changed us, he empowers us, and he loves us.

The same Spirit that raised Jesus from the dead is now in us who believe. Through faith in Jesus's life and death, we are cleansed from all unrighteousness and become holy dwelling places of God. God will not dwell in unholy people. But because of Jesus's work, we are declared righteous and holy by faith in Jesus. And now God's Spirit dwells in all those who are his (Rom. 8:9–11).

We now have the presence and power in us that spoke the world into existence, flooded the earth, parted the Red Sea, and empowered Jesus to preach, heal the sick, raise the dead, and cast out demons. We have the power that overcomes Satan, sin, and death.

This is what the gospel is and what the gospel does.

The gospel is the good news of the life, death, burial, and resurrection of Jesus, who is King. The gospel saves and brings God's rule into our lives (his kingdom) in order to bring the good news of his power into the world. The gospel changes us from the inside out and spreads through our lives and lips to the world by his Spirit.

This is the gospel that is the power of God for salvation to all who believe. This is what we have been saved by.

So what have we been saved from?

Saved From

Jesus lived the perfect life of obedience so we could be saved from striving to live that life on our own. God declares us to be righteous, not because of any work we have done, but because of the work Jesus did. We can rest from working to measure up to perfection. We can cease striving to be perfect by our own strength and efforts. We can rest in the life of Jesus lived on our behalf.

Jesus overcame Satan's temptation and wants to extend his ruling power in our lives and through our lives so we also can be saved from Satan's lies and power. Jesus came to set the captives free from slavery to Satan and sin.

Jesus died in our place to save us from the wrath of God and the penalty of sin, which is spiritual, relational, and physical death. He saves us from spiritual death and makes us alive in Christ. He atones for our guilt and removes our shame. He reconciles us to God so that we can also be reconciled to one another. And ultimately, though our bodies will fail and die, he will give us glorified resurrection bodies that will live forever.

Jesus ascended into heaven and saves us from living in the depths of sin by raising us and seating us with him in the heavenly realms. We were poor and lowly, but now we are co-heirs with Christ, sharing in his eternal blessings. We are blessed with every spiritual blessing in Christ Jesus.

And he sends his Spirit to give us new birth—a new life. He saves us from our old life of sin and identity in Adam to a new life with a new identity, a new purpose, and a new power. Anyone who is in Christ is a new creation. Not only are we declared righteous, but we also can live righteous lives. Not only are we called holy, but we also can live as God's holy people. We are new! We are alive! We are free! We are no longer slaves to sin, but are now slaves to righteousness—slaves to what is truly living!

And all of this is a gift. It is all by grace. "For by grace you have been saved through faith. And this is not your own doing; it is the gift of God, not a result of works, so that no one may boast (Eph. 2:8–9).

We receive it all by grace *through faith.*

So what does it mean to be saved through faith? What does faith have to do with all this?

6

WHAT'S FAITH GOT TO DO WITH IT?

In the true story, we see the macro picture of God's power to save. It is God's story. In it, we come to know the overarching good news. And the entire story points to Jesus. He is at the heart of the gospel. Apart from Jesus's life, death, burial, and resurrection, there is no good news.

So if it's all God's story, accomplished by God's power through the person and work of Jesus Christ, what role do we have? Do we do anything? If so, what are we supposed to do?

Believe.

When Jesus was asked, "What must we do, to be doing the

works of God?" he responded, "This is the work of God, that you believe in him whom he has sent" (John 6:28–29).

Paul reminded the Christians in Ephesus: "For by grace you have been saved through faith. And this is not your own doing; it is the gift of God, not a result of works, so that no one may boast" (Eph. 2:8–9).

The work we are called to do is to rest from our own work to make ourselves right with God and believe in the work of Jesus on our behalf.

We are saved by faith in Jesus's work, not our own.

We all live by faith in someone or something. And everything that we are and do is a result of what we believe. Our behaviors are the tangible expression of our beliefs.

The Results of Unbelief

Adam and Eve began their lives as image bearers of God, free to love and serve him and others as a picture of what God is truly like. However, instead of believing God's word and trusting in his work, they believed the lie of the Devil and trusted instead in his word and their own work. As a result of trusting in the wrong story—a false story—they experienced the rotten fruit of their misplaced faith. Sin affected every part of their being and every behavior in which they engaged. As a result, they experienced guilt, shame, and fear.

What we believe, and whom we believe in, produces something. James says, "Faith by itself, if it does not have works, is dead" (James 2:17). True faith produces works. And your works reveal what your faith is in. If your faith is in God's word and work, that faith saves, and as a result, your works look like God's. If your faith is in someone or something else, it is evident that it is not in God—so your works are ungodly.

I remember the day I heard yelling and screaming sifting up through the floorboards of our home. I ran down the stairs to find out the source of the commotion. In our dining room, I found my children angrily yelling at each other over a game of Chutes and Ladders.

I immediately shouted, "What's going on?"

"She cheated," Caleb yelled, pointing at Haylee.

"He tore the player's head off!" Haylee shouted back.

Maggie, who was five at the time, was sitting in the middle of the table, watching the commotion.

This went on for a few more rounds until I said: "I need to know what happened here. One at a time. Caleb, did you tear the head off the player?" I looked at a headless cardboard player in his hand. As I did, Caleb disappeared into his shirt. He did "The Turtle," as I like to call it. He pulled his shirt down over his knees and pulled the neck hole over his head so that all I could see was a shirtball with some hair poking through the top.

Caleb was hiding—in shame.

Two things were going on in that moment. First, Caleb knew he had done wrong, and his response was to cover up. He was acting on his faith. His first act of faith was to believe his performance in the game determined his significance. Clearly his performance had not been going well, which led to a head-less game piece. Caleb's second act of faith was clear in how he responded to his first act—by hiding. He hid because he felt shame about the inadequacy of his works, but he continued to trust his work to cover himself. Both were sins because both had to do with unbelief or wrong belief.

All sin is a result of unbelief in God—particularly unbelief in Jesus and his work.

Caleb's beliefs led to his behavior—first the decapitation, then the hiding.

The Problem

I've found when we aim to help our children or our friends experience change in their lives, too often we go after just the behavior, not the belief. As a result, we try to use the consequences of sin to get people to not sin.

I've observed this plenty of times in my parenting. I've also seen this with well-intentioned Christians. Instead of going after the wrong belief beneath the sin—the sin under the sin—we emphasize the consequences of sin to curb behavior.

For instance, in the incident mentioned above, I could have tried to use shame (a consequence of sin) to deal with the sin itself. I could have said: "How could you do that? You know better, Caleb!" I even could have gone so far as to say, "You should be ashamed of yourself!"

Remember, it is by *grace* that we are saved by *faith*, not by works. So when we sin, we don't go after works or even the results of our sin to rescue or change us. We need to address our faith and ask what we are believing and what we should believe.

We won't help people stop sinning by using the consequences of their sin to motivate them. In fact, when we do this, we just end up teaching them how to sin in other ways. If we don't lead them to repent and believe in God and the work of Jesus, we are only leading them to look elsewhere for their salvation—trusting in someone or something more than God's word and work.

For instance, think about why some people lie. Some want others to think highly of them, so they do anything to save face, including telling falsehoods. If you catch such a person in a lie and say, "Shame on you! What would people think of you if they knew you were a liar?" you are actually encouraging him, feeding his motive for sinning all the more. He has bought into the idea that he must present a false self if he is to be accepted. Now he is determined to become a better deceiver in order to never be found out.

Notice that when God pursued Adam and Eve in the garden

after they sinned, he didn't say, "Shame on you!" They were already experiencing plenty of shame for their sin. Instead, he asked where they were and why they felt the need to hide.

He was going after their beliefs as revealed through their actions.

God knew where they were and what they had done. He was not clueless. He wanted them to confess what had led them to hide. That's why he also asked them, "Who told you you were naked?" (Gen. 3:11). In other words: "Whose word about you were you believing? Mine or another's?" It was their distrust of God—their unbelief in his word—that led them to trust in self in the first place. And it was their ongoing unbelief in God that led them to continue running away from him. The way out was not to hide from God and trust in self-saving methods even more. The way out was to repent, turn back to God in faith, and receive grace, forgiveness, reconciliation, and restoration.

This is the work that we are to do—repent from wrong belief and turn to God in belief—belief in the gospel. It is by grace you have been saved *through faith*.

In the moment I confronted Caleb, I knew he was hiding because he was putting his faith in himself and his own behaviors. He felt the need to cover up because his own work was insufficient. So I called him to come out of hiding and go to Jesus in faith.

Caleb's not alone, is he? You've done "The Turtle" as well. Oh, maybe not inside of a shirt, but likely under the façade of religion, materialism, workaholism, or other forms of hiding. We've all found ways to hide our sense of inadequacy and shame. But we don't have to stay in hiding.

"Caleb, you don't need to hide," I said to him. "You don't need to cover up. Remember, Jesus died on the cross for your sins. I know you feel ashamed for what you've done. That's what we feel when we sin. But you don't have to keep hiding.

Go to Jesus. Come out of hiding and believe that he died for you and can take your shame away."

I continued to call him to turn to Jesus.

Eventually, I saw an eyeball peaking out of the shirt's neck hole, then two, then a nose—and then his whole head appeared as he leaped toward me to wrap his arms around my neck. "I'm sorry, Dad! I ripped his head off."

You know someone is coming out of hiding when he is able to confess his sin out loud. So at that moment, I reminded Caleb again that we don't have to hide when we sin. We can run to Jesus in faith that he already died to pay for our sin and remove our shame.

"I told you so!" Haylee exclaimed. "I told you he did it."

More gospel work to be done.

"Haylee, you don't need to blame," I said. "That is what we do when we want to make ourselves feel more loved or accepted by God. We feel like we have to put others down so we look better."

"But, he did it, Dad! He ripped the guy's head off," she replied.

"I know, but he doesn't need you to point the finger at him. He doesn't need you to blame him. Caleb felt shame for his sin and needed Jesus to remove it. You, on the other hand, often want to point the finger in blame."

Haylee is our firstborn, so her sense of righteousness often comes from performing better than her siblings. The only problem is that the standard isn't her siblings. The standard is Jesus. And I know she falls short of that. She knows it too. That is why she sets another standard that she can attain. So in her unbelief—which is actually just belief in her own standard of righteousness—she moves quickly to blame others in order to deal with her own sense of inadequacy. She feels righteous when others are seen as unrighteous next to her.

Sound familiar?

"Haylee, I want to remind you also that Jesus took the blame for Caleb's sin *and* yours [I knew she had cheated]. Caleb can't handle the weight of sin. Neither can you. Only Jesus can. That is why he died for it on the cross. He died for both of you. Instead of pointing your finger at Caleb, I want you to point at Jesus as the one who took the blame. Jesus took the blame for Caleb's sin, as well as your sin, on the cross. You need to look to Jesus as much as Caleb does."

She quickly realized what she had done. With big tears, she immediately said: "I'm sorry, Dad! Why do I always do this?"

I responded: "Because you forget, sweetie. You forget what Jesus has done for you. You're not alone. We all forget. That is why we continue to sin. But remember, he died for your sins. He died to forgive you and Caleb from every sin you've ever committed and every sin you will ever commit. We don't have to take the blame for our sin. And we don't need to blame others, because Jesus took the blame."

We all stopped and prayed together, thanking God once again for Jesus.

What am I doing? I am training my children to put their faith in Jesus, not themselves.

I am training them in the work they are to do.

This work is to believe—to believe the gospel.

If I don't teach Caleb that he doesn't need to hide, he will become a master deceiver to keep up the image that all is well with him. But if I teach him that the gospel frees him to confess his sin and experience times of healing and refreshing in his soul, he will grow in his faith in Jesus, which, in turn, will also train him to not need to earn his approval through his performance. As parents, Jayne and I have learned to celebrate Caleb confessing his sin instead of covering it up as an affirmation of his growing faith in the gospel.

A gospel-fluent community that is growing in faith in the gospel is evidenced by people confessing their sins to one another regularly.

And if I don't teach Haylee that Jesus took the blame for her sin, she will either point her finger at herself, leading to self-hatred, or point it at others. In either case, she will be looking for an atoning sacrifice for sin in the wrong place. Many people experience deep depression or engage in self-hurt through cutting, eating disorders, and even suicide because they keep looking to themselves for atonement. Others live with deep-rooted bitterness and hatred toward others. I want Haylee to be eager to go to Jesus so that he can atone for her sin and help her forgive the sins committed against her by others.

A gospel-fluent community that is growing in confidence that Jesus fully atoned for our sins extends grace and forgiveness to one another.

It is by grace—the gift of God in Jesus—that you are saved from the consequences and control of sin. And it is through faith—belief in Jesus's work on our behalf.

Every sinful attitude, motive, thought, or action is a result of unbelief in God's word and work. Both Caleb and Haylee were engaging in unbelief, which led Haylee to cheat and blame, and Caleb to decapitate a game piece and hide.

Caleb and Haylee were guilty of unbelief—just as our first parents were.

Paul teaches in Romans 1:18–32 that we all, like Adam and Eve and all their descendants, have exchanged the truth of God for a lie and have worshiped the creation instead of the Creator. We put our faith in the things God has made or the things we can do instead of God. God gives us over to our wrong belief and lets it produce in us what all idolatry produces—sin, brokenness, perversion, and pain. He does this so that we will see the wretchedness of sin and turn back to him as the one who forgives our sin, cleanses us from unrighteousness, and heals our brokenness.

The gospel is not just the power of God to save, but also the revelation of God that we need to be saved and that the only one who can save us is Jesus.

The Spirit's job is to reveal to us our unbelief, grant us repentance, and lead us to know and believe in Jesus.

That is the work we do. We turn from unbelief to belief in Jesus.

The Truth of God Revealed

Unbelief can take several forms: (1) we don't believe because we lack the truth about God; (2) we believe lies about God; or (3) we fail to put our faith in what we know to be true of God.

God Unknown

First, many don't know who God really is. They don't know what he is like or what he has done for us. A person can't believe in God if he or she is unaware of the truths about God.

There is no salvation—no transformation—apart from knowing God. Jesus said in John 17:3, "And this is eternal life, that they *know* you the only true God, and Jesus Christ whom you have sent." This knowing isn't only knowledge of the truths *about* God. It is also an intimate acquaintance *with* God.

One of the reasons Jesus came—and one of the reasons why the gospel is such good news—was to reveal the truth about God and to bring us into relationship with him. In John 14:6–7, Jesus said: "I am the way, and the *truth*, and the life. No one comes to the Father except through me. If you had known me, you would have known my Father also. From now on you do know him and have seen him."

Philip, one of Jesus's disciples, responded to him by saying,

"Lord, show us the Father, and it is enough for us." Jesus replied: "Have I been with you so long, and you still do not know me, Philip? Whoever has seen me has seen the Father" (John 14:8–9). Philip didn't get it. He had already seen God. God was with him in the flesh—in the body of Jesus. Jesus is the image of the invisible God—the fullness of deity in bodily form (Col. 1:15, 19).

If you want to know what God is like, look at Jesus.

That is why Jesus began this discussion with his disciples by saying, "Believe in God; believe also in me" (John 14:1).

It comes down to faith.

What do you believe about God? What do you believe he is like? What do you believe he has done?

In the gospel, we have the revelation of what God is like and what God has done. God is revealed through Jesus's life, Jesus's ministry, Jesus's death, and Jesus's resurrection.

To believe the gospel is to believe in who God is and what God does, as revealed in the person and work of Jesus Christ. And you can know if you are believing rightly because if you are, your behavior will be righteous. It will resemble Jesus's character and way of life. Your behavior reveals your beliefs. As Jesus says in John 14:12, "Truly, truly, I say to you, whoever believes in me will also do the works that I do."

Another way to think about this is that you reflect and resemble who or what you worship. Just as Jesus's works revealed what God is like, so our works reveal the object of our worship—they are an outward expression of the god we are worshiping at the moment.

Are you forgiving toward others who sin against you, or do you hold grudges and resent others? Do you know and put your faith in the God who forgives or in one who withholds forgiveness?

Are you generous with your time, talents, and treasures, or

do you hold and hoard what you have? Do you know and put your faith in the One who generously gave you his one and only Son, or are you trusting in another god?

Do you have peace in the midst of struggle, or do you live in a constant state of fear and anxiety?

You worship either a sovereign, powerful God or an ineffectual, weak god.

Your life reveals your faith in the god you worship because what you believe shows up in your behaviors.

What is your God like? What do you believe about God?

Growing in gospel fluency requires growing in our knowledge of God as he is revealed in and through Jesus Christ.

Lies Believed

Second, in some cases, our unbelief involves believing lies about God.

Satan deceived Adam and Eve into believing lies about God, and we regularly buy into his lies as well. We might know certain truths about God, but fail to believe those truths because we are deceived into believing lies.

Tim Chester, in his book *You Can Change*, asserts that underlying every sinful behavior and negative emotion is a failure to believe a truth about God. He then suggests four liberating truths as a good diagnostic tool for addressing sin in our lives:

1. God is great—so we do not have to be in control.
2. God is glorious—so we do not have to fear others.
3. God is good—so we do not have to look elsewhere.
4. God is gracious—so we do not have to prove ourselves.[1]

Let's take the first truth as an example: If we believe God is great—that he is in control—then we can trust him and be free

---

1. Tim Chester, *You Can Change: God's Transforming Power for Our Sinful Behavior and Negative Emotions* (Wheaton, IL: Crossway, 2010), 80.

from the need to take control or manipulate situations. On the other hand, if we feel anxious or have an urge to take control, it is because we have believed the lie that God is *not* great—that he's not really powerful and in control—so *we* have to be. In the gospel, we see just how great God is as he overcomes every enemy we face, including death.

Jesus came to dispel the lies. Regularly, we hear Jesus say, "*Truly, truly I say . . .*" He is replacing the lies we believe with the truths of God. Not only does he proclaim those truths verbally, but he is also the ultimate example and display of those truths.

Growing in gospel fluency requires regularly replacing lies we have believed with the truths of God revealed in Jesus. One of the reasons God sent his Spirit to us was to reveal the lies and help us believe the truth about God. I regularly invite God's Spirit to do this in my life. You can too.

Living in Unbelief

Third, we often say we believe something to be true about God, but our lives show that we don't actually believe it. We know a truth we should believe, but in actuality, we don't.

For instance, we profess belief in a God who forgives our sins through faith in the death of Jesus, but we continue to believe we need to behave better in order to make up for what we've done. When we do this, we are living in unbelief in the gospel.

I met with a young man many times to help him believe and receive God's gracious forgiveness through faith in Jesus. At one time, he told me he had committed so many heinous sins that he didn't believe God could forgive him. I kept affirming that God's power is greater than his sin, that his grace is sufficient. So one day he told me many of the things he had done. He was right. They were horrible.

"So you think God can forgive all that?" he asked.

"Yes, of course I do," I replied. "I'm certain. In fact, your belief that he can't is your expression that you believe your works are more powerful than God. Your pride led you to sin, and that same pride is leading you to believe your sin is more powerful than God's grace, forgiveness, and power. Your sin can't defeat God's grace, brother! He is greater than you, and his grace is greater than your sin."

What work did this young man need to do? He needed to repent and believe the gospel.

The work we do is believe. We are to believe God. We must believe his word and trust in his work.

I recently was painting one of my rental homes along with this man, and he expressed how he is growing in belief. He still slips in and out of belief that God's grace is sufficient for his sin, but the time lapses from unbelief to belief are growing shorter. As a result, his joy in Christ is growing.

The gospel is the power of God to save us, not only because our sin of unbelief is forgiven through Jesus's death on the cross, but also because in the gospel we come to know and believe the liberating truths of God revealed in Jesus Christ. And through believing those truths, the lies we've believed are dispelled and the truth sets us free to really live.

So what do you believe?

The gospel won't fluently come out of you to others unless it's changed you first.

So let's start with the gospel in you.

PART 3

THE GOSPEL IN ME

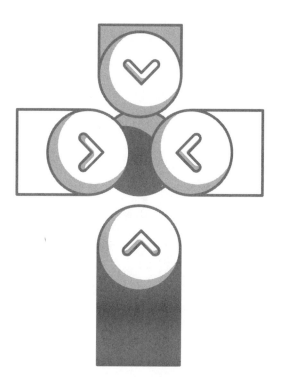

7

GOOD NEWS TO ME

I'm often asked why it's so hard for many people to talk to others about Jesus. I'm quick to reply that one of the main reasons is that we are in a spiritual battle, and the Evil One does not want people to hear the news that can set them free from his destructive rule and enslavement. I am convinced that demonic forces are regularly seeking to instill fear into Christians—fear of being rejected; fear of saying the wrong thing; and even fear that they will do something that might prevent someone from coming to faith in Jesus.

I also believe many people just feel inadequate and ill-equipped to share the truth about Jesus. They believe they need more training and more information. In some cases, this is true.

That's why I've trained thousands of people in sharing the gospel and why I am writing this book. I'm all about training people.

However, I have come to believe that the main reason people don't talk about Jesus is not that they lack training. I am convinced it is that they lack love.

People need heart change—not just once, but over and over again, because their love grows cold. People need to be deeply affected by the incredible news of Jesus on a daily basis. What affects you greatly creates in you great affections. And those affections lead you to express verbally and physically what you love most, because you talk about what you love. Furthermore, you love what you talk about. And we all talk about what most affects us—what most powerfully works to create change in our lives.

You Talk about What You Love

"She is beautiful! I love her smile and the way her eyes light up when she laughs."

I couldn't stop talking about Jayne. I was on an overnight hiking excursion with Sam, the pastor of our church. I was serving as the youth pastor, my first full-time position since graduating from college. I had been in Seattle for only a short time when I met her. She stopped by my house with a friend of hers who attended our church, and as I watched her walk up the sidewalk to the porch, it seemed as if God whispered, "That's going to be your wife." I wasn't sure if that was a wishful dream or if it was God. Regardless, I couldn't get her off my mind.

Jayne and I had been seeing each other for about a month, and all I could do was talk about how wonderful she was. "She loves Jesus! And she has a great dad who loves the Lord as well. He's a great man! He loves to laugh. His whole face lights up when he does! In fact, she's a lot like him. Her face lights up when she laughs as well. She's amazing! I love being with her!"

"All right, all right, it's obvious you love the girl. Marry her!" Sam exclaimed. He was getting tired of hearing about her constantly, but I couldn't help it. I was in love!

You talk about what you love. Everyone does.

First-time parents are constantly posting pictures of their newborns, capturing everything on video, and documenting every detail on social media: "We changed her first diaper!"; "He smiled for the first time at 9:05 a.m. Tuesday"; and "He started to crawl!" It's actually funny to be Facebook friends with first-time parents. At some point, I want to say: "He's a human. Of course he's going to do those things. Most every human who has ever existed has eventually done those things. It's what humans do. Your kid isn't *that* special!" Of course, I never do that, because Jayne and I did the exact same thing with our kids. We constantly took pictures, shot video, and documented every move. We talked about our kids to everyone. Its what you do when you love someone or something.

Do you know people who love sports? You know it if they do. I love the Seahawks, Seattle's professional football team, and you'd know that if you hung out with me for a few days. Do you know people who love finding a good deal? I'm sure you hear about it when they do. What about work? People who love their work talk about it a lot.

Jesus said that it is out of the overflow of the heart that the mouth speaks (Luke 6:45). What comes out of your heart displays what's in it and what has captured it.

Do you talk about Jesus? Has he captured your heart? Do you love him?

When you come to know and experience the love God has for us in Jesus; when you realize that God loved us so much that he was willing to suffer and die for our sins, even though we were his enemies; when you meet Jesus and experience him pouring out his Spirit into your heart, filling you with himself and his love, you can't contain it. You have to talk about it!

The gospel is incredible! The word *gospel* literally means "good news." Is it good news to you?

What do you get most excited about? What has most captured your affections? Be honest for a moment. What is it? Who is it? And why has it or he or she captured your heart?

And if your affections have been captured, how have you been affected? What do you do in light of your heart being captured?

Most importantly, has Jesus captured your affections? Why or why not? Are you impressed with him?

It will show, you know. If he has captured your affections, you will not be able to stop talking about him.

"What if I'm not very captured by him?" you might be asking yourself. "What if my affections are much stronger for lesser things?"

Well, my hope is that this book will stir up your affections more. That is one of the reasons I talk and write about Jesus so much. I'm convinced many are not aware of how great he is and how amazing his love and grace are to us. So I talk about him. I want people to know those things.

You Love What You Talk About

Another reason I talk about Jesus is that I've found you not only talk about what you love, but you also love what you talk about.

Sometimes our love grows cold. Our hearts lose affection. We forget what we have, so we drift from what we love.

I found this to be true in my marriage. Yes, I did marry that beautiful twenty-year-old blonde whom I couldn't stop talking about on that hiking trip. Jayne and I have been married for more than twenty-three years at the time of this writing. And she is more beautiful to me now than ever.

However, there have been days, even weeks or months, in our marriage when I forgot her beauty. I haven't always cherished her. My affections have not always been stirred up for her. In fact, there was a season when my love for ministry and work rivaled my love for Jayne. During that time, I didn't talk about her in the same way as I did along the trail with Sam.

So what did I do when I realized what had happened?

I started pursuing her again. I remembered what I loved about her. I went back to that day when I met her and my heart was caught off guard and captured. I reminded myself and others how beautiful, godly, wise, and amazing this woman I married is. I remembered how unworthy and blessed I was to have received such an incredible gift as Jayne. I thanked God for her every day—sometimes many times throughout a day. I started watching her more closely, paying attention to her words, her movements, her acts of kindness, her smile, and her tireless servant's heart that gives so much to me, our children, and countless others in need regularly.

And I was captured once again. I still am. Even as I am writing, my heart is swelling up with affection for my lovely bride. She is amazing! I could go on and on.

I've discovered that you love most what you talk about most.

What do you talk about most?

If you lack love for Jesus and want your love for him to grow, start talking about how amazing he is. Talk to yourself about him. By the way, you won't be alone in this venture because he sent his Spirit to tell you what is true, good, and amazing about him. The Holy Spirit is the best at bragging on Jesus because he has known him forever and is more impressed with him than anyone.

Just as I do with Jayne, I regularly meditate on how amazing Jesus is, and as I do, I often ask the Holy Spirit to show me more, teach me more, and remind me more of how great our incredible Savior is.

Read the Gospels[1] and watch Jesus closely. I would encourage you to read at least one Gospel a year to regularly reacquaint yourself with the love of your life. As you read, slow down and pay attention to his actions and words. Observe how well and how much he loves. Watch for his kindness and gentleness. Don't miss his gracious love for the broken, the weary, and the sinful.

Then, as the Spirit shows you more about Jesus, talk about what you see and learn. Talk to your roommate about how amazing Jesus is. Tell your friends. Speak with your children about him. The more you do, the more you will love him. And the more you love him, the more you will want to talk about him.

Never forget how he loved you first. First John 4:19 says, "We love because he first loved us." Regularly go back to that day when his love for you first showed up on the front porch of your heart. Don't forget what it was like when you were first captured by his affection for you. The Bible teaches a husband to rejoice in the wife of his youth (Prov. 5:18). It also teaches us, in regard to Jesus, to return to our first love (Rev. 2:2–7). In your thoughts, go back regularly to what life was like without Jesus, then remember how he changed your life forever.

If that has not yet happened to you, if your affections have not yet been captured by Jesus Christ, I pray that will change for you. As it does, tell others about his love.

You talk about what you love and you love what you talk about.

---

1. The biblical books of Matthew, Mark, Luke, and John.

You Talk about What Works

When I was eighteen, I had a 1977 Chevrolet Camaro. It was powered by a 350-cubic-inch, 185-horsepower V8 engine with a four-barrel carburetor. My brother, on the other hand, had a 1980 Mazda RX-7 that had been retrofitted for racing. Periodically, he and I found ourselves side by side on a long stretch of highway, racing. He would always beat me off the starting line, but I always beat him in the long run because my top speed was higher than his. So on a short track, he won. On a long track, I won. They were fast cars. They won races! They worked. So we talked about our cars and our races (not to our parents, of course, but to our friends).

Have you ever met someone who does CrossFit? Do you know a person on the Paleo Diet? What about someone who listens regularly to Dave Ramsey to order her finances?

We like to talk about what is impressive. We talk about what changes us. We talk about what works.

We were created by God to work, and in Christ Jesus, we were re-created for good works that God prepared in advance for us to do (Eph. 2:10). This is why we talk about what works.

We like things to work. And when things work well, we talk about that. We also talk about what does not work for the same reason.

Now, stop and think again about what you talk about. What works in your life? What doesn't work?

The gospel works, and it addresses what doesn't work.

It is the power of God for salvation to everyone who believes. Through the gospel, God forgives, heals, fills you with love and power, sets you free, and enables you to live an altogether different life. You know this if you believe the gospel, because if you believe it, you know how well it works. The gospel of Jesus Christ changes you. And when it changes you, you talk about it.

If we are going to be fluent in the gospel, we need to stop and reflect on how the gospel works in our lives. What has God done in you? How has he changed you? How is he at work in you right now?

Maybe you currently need the power of the gospel at work in your life. What work do you need God to do in you today? How might the gospel work to address that?

It's possible you haven't yet experienced God's power to save you. Or maybe it's been a while since you have walked in the power of the gospel to save you today. For this reason, I decided to place this section, "The Gospel in Me," before the next one, "The Gospel with Us." You won't be fluent in the gospel if the gospel isn't really good news to you yet.

I still live in the Seattle area, and on February 2, 2014, we had some good news to proclaim. Our Seahawks destroyed the Denver Broncos in the Super Bowl.

Sorry, Broncos fans. (Well, not really.)

Now, as far as I know, there were no Seahawks fan training events or "evangelism" classes on how to proclaim the crushing victory. Nobody had to hand out tracts because people were too inept to tell the story of our victory. I don't recall anybody teaching people how to draw pictures showing the growing chasm of years that separated us from the Vince Lombardi Trophy finally being bridged by Russell Wilson, Marshawn Lynch, the Legion of Boom, and the 12th Man (Seahawks fans).

No, we didn't need help telling the story of our victory. You couldn't shut us up. You still can't (even a few years later).

We had a story to tell—the Seahawks defeated Peyton Manning and all of his minions. The odds seemed to be against us: "Can anything good come from Seattle?" the media asked. But we knew all along we could win. Our Seahawks made a public spectacle out of Peyton and his Broncos. We came home with the trophy!

Seattle proclaimed the good news because it was good news. We love our Seahawks. We talk about our Seahawks. And our Seahawks worked the Broncos over. We were the champions and the Broncos were thoroughly defeated.

We talk about what we love. We love what we talk about. And we talk about what works!

We have a far greater story to tell than a football victory. We were enemies of God, hopeless and helpless, enslaved to sin and Satan, crushed daily by his destructive blows. For hundreds of years, the world needed a Savior. We needed to be set free, forgiven, and restored.

Jesus came, and it did not look good. He was from *Nazareth*, for goodness' sake! But he lived the life we couldn't. He went "undefeated" for thirty-three years. Then, on the cross, it looked as if it was over—and it was. But it wasn't a victory for evil. Jesus won as he rose again on the third day!

Sin was paid for, Satan was crushed, and death was dealt a deathblow. Jesus made a public spectacle of Satan, sin, and death, and overcame for us.

Now we are free, forgiven, loved, and more than conquerors!

Do you believe it? Do you love it? Do you love him?

If so, tell the world! Tell your community. Tell your friends. Tell your spouse. Tell your children. Tell your neighbor. Tell your boss. Tell your coworkers. Tell your enemies. Tell them every day. Tell everyone that love has come to town and defeated death, hatred, sickness, and sorrow!

It's good news! It's great news! It's the gospel of Jesus Christ!

It starts in you and spills out of your heart through your mouth to the world, for it's out of the overflow of your heart that your mouth speaks.

You will talk about him if you love him. If you don't, start talking about him, what's he's done, and what he's done for you, and you will love him. And you'll begin to see more and more clearly how wonderful his gospel is and how powerfully it works. As a result, you will talk about Jesus more and more.

He is the best news there is.

8

THE WAR OF THE MIND

We are at war! Bullets are flying. Bombs are dropping. The enemy is closing in. Destruction is all around. There are casualties everywhere.

But in our war, you can't see any of this. Well, you can see the effects of it all over the place in the brokenness, chaos, and pain around us, but this war is invisible.

We are not fighting one another. Our war is not against "flesh and blood, but against the rulers, against the authorities, against the cosmic powers over this present darkness, against the spiritual forces of evil in the heavenly places" (Eph. 6:12).

And we are not fighting with physical weapons. We fight what is unseen with weapons that are not wielded by human hands. Our battle is spiritual, and so are our weapons. Our weapons have divine power to set people free, destroy sinful thoughts and behaviors, and demolish demonic strongholds. Jesus defeated Satan, sin, and death for us so that we could be set free and empowered to overcome our enemies with the same power that filled Jesus throughout his mission and raised him from the dead on that victorious Sunday morning.

The gospel is the power of God for salvation. And our enemies are the Devil, the world, and the flesh.

The Devil is opposed to God and all that is good, right, and perfect. He pretends to have our best interests in mind, but he is dead set on destroying us. The Bible says he charades as an angel of light (2 Cor. 11:14), but in actuality, he is a roaring lion seeking those he may devour (1 Pet. 5:8). For that reason, he is also called Satan, which means "adversary."

When the Bible speaks of "the world" as an enemy, it is not referring to the blue and green rotating ball called Earth that we live on. The world that both James and John warn us about is the place where the rule and reign of the Devil is expressed and experienced (James 4:4; 1 John 2:15–17). Satan is called the god of this world, referring to his evil reign of darkness and destruction. In this case, the world is everything that stands against the rule and reign of God.

The flesh is that part of us that orients itself to self-worship and self-dependency. It intends to keep us from doing God's will. Like Satan and the world, the flesh is opposed to God. Romans 8:7–8 says, "The mind that is set on the flesh is hostile to God, for it does not submit to God's law; indeed, it cannot. Those who are in the flesh cannot please God."

To be clear, those who are *in the flesh* are those who have not yet been saved—they have yet to experience spiritual regeneration brought about by the Spirit of God through faith in the person and work of Jesus Christ. By contrast, Paul goes on to say, referring to those who belong to Christ: "You, how-ever, are not in the flesh but in the Spirit, if in fact the Spirit of God dwells in you. Anyone who does not have the Spirit of Christ does not belong to him" (Rom. 8:9). Those who belong to Christ have been set free and given power to overcome the flesh by setting their minds on the Spirit, whose job it is to bring the truths of Jesus and the victory of Jesus to bear on the spiritual battle we are facing (vv. 1–6). That doesn't mean that we don't battle the flesh, which is our old nature. It just means that we are no longer *in* the flesh—no longer the old person we once were.

The Devil screams out: "God is evil. I hate him and I will do everything to oppose him and destroy what he has made."

The world screams out: "This world is best without God, and you are best when it's all about you."

And the flesh screams out: "I don't need God because I am god. It's all about me and it's all dependent upon me."

So what are we to do in this battle? The Bible tells us to (1) take our thoughts captive and examine them, (2) bring them into submission, (3) consider the fruit, and then (4) fight with gospel truths.

Capture and Examine Your Thoughts

We overcome the enemies of God by taking every thought cap-tive to obey Christ (2 Cor. 10:5). To take something captive is to take control of it and put it in a controlled environment. It is like subduing a ferocious animal and putting it in a cage. This is what we regularly need to do with our thoughts—subdue them, capture them, and put them in a mental cage. Then we need to take a close look at them and consider what we're thinking and why. What is going through your mind? What do you regularly hear spoken in your head? What are you believing about God, his work in Jesus, others, yourself, and what you should do?

Take each thought captive to obey Christ. Another way of saying this is, make sure that what you are thinking lines up with what is true of Jesus and of your new life in him. Make sure it conforms to the truths of the gospel.

This is why it is so important to know the gospel, rehearse it in our minds, and remember it. We cannot defeat the enemies of our souls without becoming more gospel fluent. And part of growing in gospel fluency is learning how to recognize what is not from God—what is not in line with the truths of the gospel.

So how do you know if what you're thinking lines up with what is true in the gospel?

Well, remember that the gospel literally means "good news." So ask yourself: "Is this good news that I'm thinking? Is it tearing God down or lifting him up? Is it tearing others down or building them up? Is it tearing me down or encouraging, exhorting, or equipping me?"

The enemy of our souls brings to our minds thoughts and words that are lies about God, while also accusing us, tempting us, and dividing and isolating us. Some of the *lies* you might hear are:

- God doesn't really love you.
- He's out to get you and destroy your life.
- God has left you. You're all alone and he doesn't care. You're not that important to him.
- Besides, even if he did love you, he couldn't help you. He's not that powerful.
- He can't be everywhere, you know.
- And even if he could, the stuff you're dealing with doesn't matter to him.

There are more lies than I have room to write, because Satan is the master of lies about God and his work. He has been doing this since the beginning. He doesn't want you to trust God or depend on him, so he lies about God and his work. The world gladly accepts these lies and passes them on, and since we grow up in a broken world, we all buy into many lies and rehearse them in our minds.

One good way to learn how to discern the truth from a lie is to continue reading Scripture. If what you hear disagrees with the Bible, it's a lie.

Satan also *accuses*:

- You really blew it this time! You should be ashamed of yourself.
- It shouldn't surprise you, however; you always do stuff like that. You're such a loser!
- How many more times do you have to fail to realize it?
- You're never going to amount to much of anything.
- It's all because you're a filthy sinner. It's what you do. You're no saint, that's for sure.

He loves to tear us down with accusations. And most often he tries to deny what is true of us in Christ—what Jesus has done to change us. He doesn't want us to live boldly for Jesus, so he accuses us of things that are not true of us so that we will cower in fear, guilt, and shame.

He also *tempts* us with promises of fulfillment through sinful pleasures or pursuits. He tries to convince us that God's ways are not good. And he loves to offer seductive shortcuts to fulfill our longings and desires. He often tries to make sin look attractive to lure our hearts away from obeying God:

- Look at this image—you know it will make you feel powerful or desired or aroused.
- Go ahead, take one more drink. It will make all your troubles go away.
- God knows this is enjoyable. He just doesn't want you to have any fun.

- You deserve better. You've worked so hard, what's wrong with a little reward?
- You know you need that. And if you get it, everything will change for you.

The temptations come in all forms, but every one of them is an empty promise leading to an unfulfilled longing. Satan tries to convince us that there is a shortcut to deep fulfillment and satisfaction outside of God and his ways.

Have you heard these lies, accusations, and temptations?

The enemy also loves to *divide* and *isolate* through gossip, slander, and bitterness:

- Go ahead, say it. You know it's true.
- Everyone else should know how much they've messed up as well.
- Besides, think about how good it'll make you feel to be seen as better than them!
- Put some spin on this one. Make the story a little juicier. People love scandal.
- They really did hurt you! They deserve to suffer for that. Don't let it go.
- They should pay. It's about time they got what was coming to them!

The means vary, but our enemy loves to turn us against one another. He loves to erode our trust and give us reasons to separate or divide. And one of his greatest schemes is to isolate us as he does it. He wants us alone so he can pick us off one by one with no one around to encourage us or speak the truths of Jesus into our lives.

Watch out for the Devil's schemes. In all of them, our enemy is dead set on our destruction.

The first step is to capture the thought and examine it. Train yourself to regularly stop and closely examine what you are thinking, feeling, or believing in light of the truths of the gospel.

Bring the Thought into Submission

Once you've captured the thought, ask the Spirit to help you bring it into submission to Jesus. In other words, examine it enough to see if it lines up with what is true of God and his work in and through Jesus, and what is true of you as a result of your faith in Jesus.

This is one of the reasons God sent his Spirit to us—to guide us into all truth, teach us what is true of Jesus, and regularly witness to us about these truths. He also convicts us of any unbelief in Jesus and reveals the lies we have believed (John 14–16).

When I first started to become aware of my need to grow in gospel fluency, this was not a natural process for me. I had to practice preaching the gospel to myself first. I regularly rehearsed the truths of the gospel at the beginning of my day:

- God is perfect. Jesus lived perfectly for me. He is my righteousness.
- God loves me. Jesus died for my sins. I am loved and forgiven.
- God is powerful and mighty. Jesus rose from the dead. I am more than a conqueror in him.
- God is alive and present and with me. He sent his Spirit to be with me and in me. I am not alone or without the power to overcome.
- God is for me and not against me.

Then, throughout my day, I had to preach the gospel to myself over and over again. I didn't do this alone. I asked the Holy Spirit to teach me, encourage me, remind me of what is true of Jesus, and convict and correct me when I was going the wrong way in my heart and mind.

I still do this. Every day, I invite the Holy Spirit to preach the truths of Jesus to my heart all day long: "Holy Spirit, remind me of Jesus. Keep teaching me all that he is and all that he has done, is doing, and will do. And remind me who I am in Christ as a result. I need your witness. I need your help. I need your guidance. I need your power. I need your truth!"

As I become aware of a thought, emotion, or motive, I ask myself some or all of these questions:

- Is this really true? Or is it a lie?
- Is this from God or someone else?
- Does this sound like the Devil's accusation or the Spirit's conviction?
- Does it line up with the gospel of Jesus Christ?
- What am I hoping in right now? What do I believe this hope promises to give me?
- Why am I considering this behavior? What will be its outcome?
- In all of this, what is true of Jesus? What is true of who I am in him?
- How did Jesus do better for me? How did he speak a better word over me?
- What about Jesus do I need to remember and believe right now?

If you are going to grow in gospel fluency, you need to do the same. Just as in learning a language, you need to capture and examine your thoughts to see if they line up with the gospel, then bring them into submission to Christ by regularly rehearsing the truths of the gospel to yourself over and over again.

Remember, you don't have to do this alone. You have the Spirit of God with you to develop you in the gospel. Invite him to help you, to teach you, to bring to your mind all that is true of Jesus. You should also be in community with others who know and love Jesus, who can help you in the battle. Later in the book, we're going to look at how to practice this through immersion in a gospel community.

Consider the Fruit

The Spirit's job is to direct us to the truths of Jesus. In so doing, he also brings about the fruit that resembles the life of Jesus. Paul said that those who walk with the Spirit experience the fruit of the Spirit, which is "love, joy, peace, patience, kindness, goodness, faithfulness, gentleness, self-control" (Gal. 5:16, 22–23). The work of the flesh, on the other hand, produces what is contrary to Jesus, such as "sexual immorality, impurity, sensuality, idolatry [making a good thing a god-thing], sorcery, enmity, strife, jealousy, fits of anger, rivalries, dissensions, divisions, envy, drunkenness, orgies, and things like these" (vv. 19–21).

One of the ways we fight the war of the mind is by considering the fruit we're presently experiencing or the fruit we would experience if we engaged a particular thought or suggested action. When I am not experiencing the fruit of the Spirit or my life is not resembling the life of Jesus, then clearly my mind is not set on the Spirit. That means my mind is not in submission to Christ. Whatever is in submission to Jesus Christ begins to look like Jesus and the fruit of the Spirit.

I learned how to do this during a very difficult season of my life. I had been leading the student ministry at a fairly large church for a while when I began to lose the trust of my team. I did my best to win back their favor and to posture myself in such a way as to regain their trust. Things only got worse. At one point, the executive pastor began to join me in my staff meetings to evaluate my leadership effectiveness.

As I began to question my identity and calling, I slipped into a downward spiral of depression. My thoughts were self-loathing and self-defeating. I was filled with condemnation and an ongoing fear of failure. I also heard regular lies and accusations, including:

- If you don't succeed at this, you will never get to do ministry again—not just here, but anywhere!
- Everyone is watching you.
- They will all know you're a failure.

Fear was controlling me. It was clear I was not free. This was *not* the fruit of the Spirit. I had to pray during my thirty-minute commute just to face the workday, and then pray on the thirty-minute drive home just to have the emotional strength to engage with my wife and our newborn. This went on for about six months.

During this time, I began to see a counselor and to meet with another godly leader at our church. They both took the time to learn my story and pay attention to what was informing my behaviors. They were the first people in my life to show me how to take captive my thoughts and bring them into submission to Jesus Christ. Previously, I had been accustomed to living like a victim to my unbelief, broken thoughts, and spiritual attacks.

As we walked through my story and my situation, I began to realize that I had come to believe that my success and people's approval were my functional justification. I believed that if I performed well and people liked me, I was good. If they disliked me or my work, I was a failure.

I believed a false gospel. My acceptance and approval were not based on God's word and work. They were all up to me and what people thought of me. I was believing a long list of lies.

This is part of the battle—coming to see where we have been duped and deceived.

I also came to see that I had a huge fear of conflict. I had learned to strive for peace in all relationships at all costs—even compromising my convictions, flattering to win approval, or withholding the truth when a person needed to hear it. I had become so fearful of man and losing others' approval or loyalty that I had compromised my own character and convictions.

I had exchanged the truths of God for lies and worshiped myself and others instead of God. I had learned to look to what I could do to gain acceptance and to people whom he had created to be my god instead of him.

Man had become big, including my perception of myself, and God had become very small in my mind.

When I slowed down to capture my thoughts, I was shocked by how distorted my view of reality had become and how enslaved I had become because of unbelief.

Fight with Gospel Truths

My mentors reminded me that in the gospel, we know that God is more powerful than the enemies of our souls. Clearly he was also more powerful than my peers and leaders. I also remember hearing the Spirit tell me I was accepted and loved, not because of my position or success in the church, but because of Jesus's position and success in living, dying, and rising again. My life was hidden with Christ in God (Col. 3:3), and I had no need to be ashamed or to live in fear.

I had worried about what others would think of me if I failed. The Spirit reminded me that ministry is not about me or dependent upon me. He reminded me that Jesus didn't just die to pay for my sin—including my present sin of looking to others to be god for me. Jesus also rose again to put to death sin's power over me. I was living in fear and I had become a slave to people's opinions, but Jesus died and rose again to set me free from that captivity.

The Spirit also reminded me that because of Jesus's work on my behalf, I am fully loved and accepted by God the Father.

I had already been given the greatest acceptance and approval there is. As I believed once again that I was loved, accepted, and approved of by God in Jesus, I could finally face losing the approval of man. As this truth sank deep into my heart, I felt a huge weight being lifted off my shoulders. It was freedom!

I was doing battle with the weapons of the gospel.

When I am teaching people how to fight with gospel truths, I introduce some cues to help them discover the aspect of the gospel they may need to press into. For instance, if someone is struggling with guilt or shame for what he has done, I encourage him to go to the cross where Jesus died and remember his words: "Father, forgive them, for they know not what they do" (Luke 23:34). We need the reminder that Jesus's death paid for all our sin, past, present, and future. He atoned for our sin, removed our guilt, and covered our shame.

If someone is struggling to overcome sin, I might encourage her to remember and believe in the resurrection, where Jesus condemned sin's power. He gives us the same power to overcome by the Spirit who raised him from the dead.

Some are dealing with feelings of inadequacy in their behavior and lean toward performance-based acceptance. If so, I direct them to remember Jesus's life, perfectly lived in their place, and the Father's words spoken over Jesus (words that are now ours in Jesus): "This is my beloved Son, with whom I am well pleased" (Matt. 3:17).

Whatever the struggle, the life, death, burial, and resurrection of Jesus give life, hope, and power. By faith in Christ, every attribute, characteristic, and blessing that belongs to Jesus is available and accessible to us as we depend on and submit to him. We are co-heirs with Christ, blessed with every spiritual blessing in the heavenly realms, and he is present and ready to give us himself and anything we need to accomplish his will (Eph. 1:3–23).

In essence, fighting with gospel truths is trusting in and putting on ourselves all that is true of Jesus, and therefore also true of us in Jesus.

Paul exhorted the church in Ephesus: "Finally, be strong in the Lord and in the strength of his might. Put on the whole armor of God, that you may be able to stand against the schemes of the devil" (Eph. 6:10–11). He then went on to describe the armor: "Stand therefore, having fastened on the belt of truth, and having put on the breastplate of righteousness, and, as shoes for your feet, having put on the readiness given by the gospel of peace. In all circumstances take up the shield of faith, with which you can extinguish all the flaming darts of the evil one; and take the helmet of salvation, and the sword of the Spirit, which is the word of God, praying at all times in the Spirit" (vv. 14–18).

We do battle by having the truths of the gospel around us like a belt, holding everything up. Our hearts are protected by the breastplate of Jesus's righteousness. We continue to believe that it is his righteousness that makes us right with God, not ours. We have a readiness—a quickness—to run from evil and to chase after obedience because we are free and unhindered by guilt, shame, and fear. Because of Jesus, our guilt is removed, our shame is covered, and our fear is demolished, for he is victorious over our enemies.

In everything you face, believe. Remember, belief is the work we are to do. We take up the shield of faith. We believe in God. We believe in all that he has accomplished for us in Jesus Christ. We trust in him for every situation. This good news is a helmet that covers our minds to protect us from the lies, accusations, and temptations we face. And we are not just on the defensive in this battle. We can and must wield the sword of the Spirit— the word of God—and the gospel of Jesus Christ to attack the schemes of the Devil. This is all accomplished with an ongoing dependence on the Spirit in prayer. The weapons alone are not enough. We must submit ourselves to the Spirit who empowers them all.

This is how we go to war.

It's important to note that my struggle didn't just go away instantly. In fact, in my newfound freedom, I still had to face the reality of my failures. I needed God's grace for what I had done, and I received it in the gospel. I also had to practice gospel-centered spiritual warfare. I had to begin regularly capturing my thoughts, looking to see the lies and accusations, standing firm on the gospel truths, putting on the gospel weapons to fight, and walking in faith through prayerful dependence on the Spirit.

As I did these things, I started to grow in fighting the good fight of the faith. I found that I could resist the Devil and he would flee (James 4:7). I began to put to death the flesh and overcome the fears of the world. Increasingly, I experienced greater freedom and greater victory. I began to see more clearly, hear from God more consistently, and walk with a newfound freedom and courage daily.

I experienced what Paul says to the church in Rome: "Do not be conformed to this world, but be transformed by the renewal of your mind, that by testing you may discern what is the will of God, what is good and acceptable and perfect" (Rom. 12:2).

If you are going to become gospel fluent, you must be prepared to go to war.

Take thoughts captive and examine them closely.

Bring them into submission.

Consider the fruit.

Then fight with gospel truths.

9

FRUIT TO ROOT

It was our day off, and I had just returned from dropping the kids off at school to find Jayne still in her blue bathrobe, drinking her morning coffee. It was clear she wasn't doing well.

Jayne was struggling with a lot of anxiety over our children. Where were they with Jesus? Were they going to surrender their lives to him? Were they safe in our neighborhood? How could we protect them? And what about school? Should they actually be going to a public school? What were they being exposed to? She was being crushed by the weight of so many concerns.

Part of our job in growing in gospel fluency is paying attention to the overflow of our hearts. What comes out in the form of thoughts, emotions, and behaviors finds its origin inside of us. Too often, we focus our attention on changing the external rather than addressing the internal. But Jesus was very clear that what defiles us proceeds from inside our hearts—our beliefs and our motives. The fruit of our lives comes from the roots of our faith. Just as a thermometer detects a fever, what we see or experience tells us about the gospel health of our hearts. So we need to learn to trace the fruit back to the root.

Over the years, I have learned to ask four key questions in progressive order when forming people in the gospel: (1) Who is God? (2) What has God done (which reveals who God is)? (3) Who am I in light of God's work? and (4) How should I live in light of who I am?

For instance, (1) Who is God? One answer is that God is love. (2) What has God done (in other words, how do I know he is love)? He sent his Son to die for me while I was still a sinner. (3) Who am I in light of God's work (in this case, his sending of his Son to die for me)? I am dearly loved by God—I am God's son. (4) How should I live in light of who I am? I should love others as God loved me.

I encourage people to apply these questions to their Bible study and to all of their discipleship processes. I do this because we all do what we do because of what we believe about (1) who God is, (2) what God has done, and (3) who we are in Christ or apart from Christ.

The roots of our faith produce the fruit of our life.

When I am seeking to discern unbelief in the gospel, I reverse the order of those questions: (1) What am I doing or experiencing right now? (2) In light of what I am doing or experiencing, what do I believe about myself? (3) What do I believe God is doing or has done? and (4) What do I believe God is like? In other words, I trace the fruit back to the root. If the fruit is not like Jesus, that is an indicator that our faith is not in him.

Remember, we're all still unbelievers in many areas of our lives (as we saw in chapter 1). We do not always believe the truths about God as revealed in the gospel; therefore, we are living in unbelief.

We still are *being* saved.

How do we know if the fruit of our lives is like Jesus?

Well, it helps to get to know what Jesus is like. This is why we need to continue to become more and more acquainted with him by reading the Scriptures, especially the Gospels, which describe how Jesus lived. Remember, Jesus said, "Truly, truly, I say to you, whoever believes in me will also do the works that I do" (John 14:12). In another place, he summed up all of the commands in this way: Love the Lord your God with all you are and love others as yourselves (Matt. 22:37–40).

The fruit of faith in Jesus is love for God and others.

The gospel makes clear that this is not something we do on our own. Through faith in Jesus, each of us is made into a pure and holy dwelling place—a temple—where God's Spirit lives. Jesus foretold that he would send the Spirit to help us know, believe in, and be connected to Jesus, so that we could bear much fruit.

As we saw in the previous chapter, the Bible says that we should examine our lives to determine whether we are producing "the works of the flesh," which are opposed to God, or "the fruit of the Spirit," which are expressions of what Jesus is like:

> Now the *works of the flesh* are evident: sexual immorality, impurity, sensuality, idolatry, sorcery, enmity, strife, jealousy, fits of anger, rivalries, dissensions, divisions, envy, drunkenness, orgies, and things like these. I warn you, as I warned you before, that those who do such things will not inherit the kingdom of God. But the *fruit of the Spirit* is love, joy, peace, patience, kindness, goodness, faithfulness, gentleness, self-control; against such things there is no law. (Gal. 5:19–23)

Clearly, Jayne was experiencing not the fruit of the Spirit, but the fruit of the flesh. She was experiencing strife, not peace. Why? Because at that moment, she was not believing the truths of the gospel.

From Fruit to Root

So I started asking Jayne the questions designed to help her see her unbelief in the gospel.[1] First, I drew a tree on a napkin and asked Jayne what she was experiencing. She said she was experiencing anxiety and fear, so I wrote *anxiety* and *fear* hanging from the tree like fruit. I also asked what she was doing or trying to do. She said she was worrying and trying to figure out how to control the situation. So I wrote down *worry* and *desire for control*—two more pieces of fruit hanging on the tree of Jayne's life (see Figure 9A on page 122).

Next, I asked her: "In light of what you are experiencing, what are you believing about yourself right now? How do you perceive who you are in this situation?"

She responded, "I am in control."

"But if you're in control," I asked, "why are you anxious? Why do you worry?"

She said: "Well, because I'm *not* in control. But I believe I have to be."

Earlier, I shared how Tim Chester teaches that beneath every sin is a failure to believe a truth about God. I'm convinced the same applies to what we believe about ourselves. Because we believe lies about God, we also believe lies about ourselves. We believe God is unloving, so we, in turn, believe we are unlovable—disposable, unwanted garbage. We believe God is not our

---

1. This was the only time I ever drew the tree for Jayne. I think that's all it took because she's a visual learner. It made a lot more sense for her to see it, not just hear it. After that, we had a visual metaphor to go back to as we worked from fruit to root over and over again. The picture also provided a way for us both to slow down and really listen to what was going on in her heart. I hope you can use the tree in a similar way for the visual learners in your life.

Savior, so we have to be the savior to our friends, our spouses, or our children.

Jayne was believing she was supposed to be in control—like God—sovereign and all-powerful. And she was believing that her worrying could actually fix everything. She believed her worrying would solve problems, but, in fact, it was creating more problems.

We all fluctuate between the extremes of believing we are demigods sent to save the world and demons who are the scum of the earth, and everything in between. And the reason we believe what we do about ourselves is because of what we believe or don't believe about God.

"What do you believe God is doing or has done, sweetheart?" I asked.

"I *feel* as if he has stopped loving me," Jayne said.

"No, I asked you what you *believe*, not just what you feel. You feel anxious and afraid, but what do you believe about what God has done."

I have found that many people don't know how to distinguish what they feel and experience from what they actually believe. In order to grow in applying the gospel to ourselves, we must learn to pay close attention to what we are believing in the moment.

"I believe he has stopped loving me. I believe he has lost control of what's going on with our children. And . . . he's abandoned me," Jayne said. I wrote these answers under the fruit, next to the right side of the tree trunk.

"And what do those beliefs tell you about what you are believing God is like?" I asked.

"He's unloving. He's impotent. He is absent," she said. I wrote all of this down too.

I have to be honest—when Jayne said God is impotent, I was a little shocked. That's a serious statement! But one thing

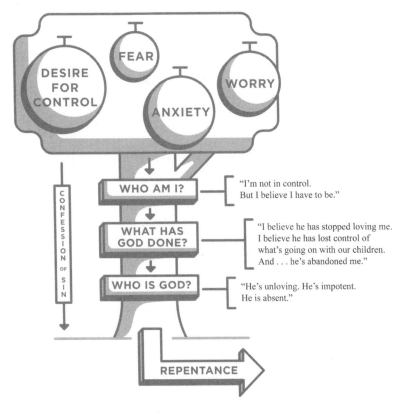

Figure 9A: Works of the Flesh

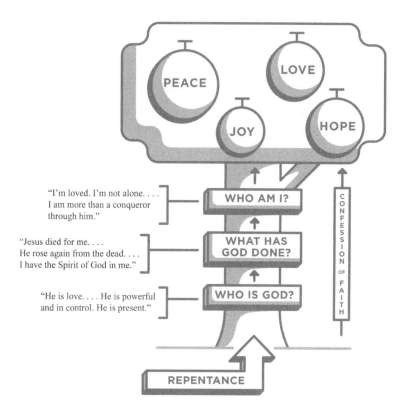

"I'm loved. I'm not alone. . . .
I am more than a conqueror
through him."

WHO AM I?

"Jesus died for me. . . .
He rose again from the dead. . . .
I have the Spirit of God in me."

WHAT HAS
GOD DONE?

"He is love. . . . He is powerful
and in control. He is present."

WHO IS GOD?

CONFESSION OF FAITH

REPENTANCE

Figure 9B: Fruit of the Spirit

I love about Jayne (among many things) is that she is honest. She is not afraid to speak out loud what is going on inside her. And she is confident that God is not surprised because she understands that he already knows what is going on inside her and he can handle it.

He knows what's going on inside you, as well. He is fully aware and not surprised. Neither is he too weak to handle your wrong beliefs about him. You can tell him what you're believing. He can handle it.

We need to learn to speak our beliefs out loud. So often, we are not even aware of what we are believing in any given moment. We just go along, living in false belief, and, as a result, we continue to engage in sinful behaviors. I am so blessed to have a friend and partner in Jayne who encourages me to speak out loud what is going on in my heart between me and God. She is in good company with the psalmists and the prophets in the Scriptures. They knew that our transformation comes partly through our verbal proclamation of our faith—speaking out loud what we are believing in the moment.

This is confession.

What was Jayne doing? She was confessing. Specifically, she was confessing her sin.

So often, when people are led to confess their sins, they only confess their sinful *behaviors*. In other words, they confess the fruit. They say: "I'm sorry I lied. Please forgive me." Or: "I looked at pornography. I know that's wrong. Please forgive me." The problem, however, is that they need to confess their sinful beliefs—the roots, the stuff below the surface that is motivating and producing their behaviors, the sin beneath the sins. All sin stems from wrong beliefs—lies we believe—and ultimately from our unbelief in Jesus. And because we generally don't go beyond the fruit to the root, we end up aiming at behavior modification instead of gospel transformation. "I'm sorry, I promise I won't do it again" or "I'm going to try harder in the future" are among our typical responses.

Typically, someone might respond to Jayne's worry and anxiety by saying something like this: "Well, don't worry. Be happy! Cheer up. It's not as bad as you think. It could be worse." The problem is that such responses don't address the real problem—the sin under the sins—and it might actually be as bad as we think, or worse. Besides, it could get worse.

In the gospel, we come to see that sin is wicked and our world is broken. We suffer and will suffer because of sin. We are not promised a pain-free, trouble-free, suffering-free existence. One of the reasons Jayne was worrying was that she knew it could be worse, but the problem was that she was looking to herself to deal with that future possibility.

This kind of response leads us to put the weight of change on ourselves or our own efforts. "I've got to stop worrying," we tell ourselves. Then we make greater self-efforts toward behavior modification. Or we end up living in denial about the real spiritual battle going on in and around us: "It's not that bad. Just think happy thoughts."

But we don't need more self-help and we don't need denial. We need deliverance.

Satan is real. Sin is bad. Death is inevitable.

We need more than ourselves and our personal efforts. We need the truth. We need the power of God to save us. We need the gospel! In the gospel, we come to know and believe that God is our forgiver, redeemer, and restorer. He has power over sin and the ability to heal us from sin's effects. When we address only the behaviors and push people to change what they do without a change in what they believe, the weight falls on us rather than God to handle the problems of the world and deal with the brokenness caused by sin.

Instead, we need to trust in God's power to change us and

change the world. Jayne needed to believe in God's love, power, and presence. She needed gospel transformation, not just behavior modification.

When Jayne saw what I had written about her beliefs, she exclaimed, "But I don't really believe that about God!"

"No, but you *have been believing* that about him," I responded. As she heard herself saying out loud what she had been believing, the Spirit immediately came alongside her to remind her of the truths she knew about God and had believed in the past.

God's Spirit is our guide, teacher, and counselor. When those of us who belong to God confess out loud what we believe, the Spirit is right there with us to convict us of our unbelief and lead us to the truth that is in Jesus. This is how God grants us repentance. He convicts us of our unbelief and leads us to believe the truth.

From Root to Fruit

Having identified the points of Jayne's unbelief, I turned the questions around: "What do you believe about God? Who is God?" I asked her. As she spoke, I wrote down her answers on the other side of the tree trunk, starting at the bottom and moving up with each question (see Figure 9B on page 123).

"He is love," she said.

"How do you know that God is love?" I asked. In essence, I was asking the second question: "What has God done to show you he is love?"

Before we move on, it is important to note how important this second question is. So often, when a Christian tries to encourage another person to believe or behave differently, he fails to proclaim the gospel—the good news about what God has done in Jesus Christ to reveal himself to us and to change us. For instance, he might say to Jayne, "Don't worry, God loves you!" That is true, but it is not enough just to say this. How do we know God loves us? And which god are we talking about? For many people in the world, God is impersonal and distant—disengaged and unconcerned with the daily stuff of our lives. So "God loves you!" doesn't mean much. We need to give others the gospel.

So I asked, "How do you know that God is love, Jayne?"

"Jesus died for me," she said.

"That's right," I said. "I want to remind you, sweetheart, of God's love for you. While you were a sinner, Christ died for you. When you were an enemy of God, he loved you enough to give his own Son for you. He loves you so much! Even when you don't trust him, he still loves you. When you're full of worry and anxiety. When you try to be god for our family instead of letting him be God. No matter what, he loves you."

Then I went back to the first question: "What else do you believe about God?" I asked.

She responded, "He is powerful and in control." Again Jayne was confessing, but this time she was confessing her faith.

"How do you know that? What has he done to show us this is true?"

"He created the world. He overcame Satan. He defeated sin. He rose again from the dead."

"That's right!" I exclaimed. "If there ever was a time when it looked as if God had lost power—had lost control—it was when Jesus was dead in a tomb. And yet, God was completely in control the entire time. He was so in control that what looked like defeat was actually victory over Satan, sin, and death! In his death, he crushed them all."

What was I doing? I was making sure Jayne's confession about God was true. And what is truth? Jesus is the truth—he is how we come to know the truths about God. As we confess and believe these truths, we are being saved, not just once, but over and over again. Jayne needed to be saved from her unbelief in that moment.

"What else do you believe, babe?" I continued.

"I believe God is with me. He's not absent. He is present."

"How do you know that?" I asked.

"Because of the Spirit. I have the Spirit of God in me."

"That's true!" I responded. "Jesus sent his Spirit to dwell in your heart. You're not alone. He is with you. And all of his love and power are available to you right now for all you're struggling with."

As we continued to speak out loud the truths of God revealed to us through the gospel, Jayne experienced a change. She was changing in the moment. She was being transformed by the renewal of her mind, just as Paul says in Romans 12:2. This wasn't just behavior modification. This was much deeper. This was gospel transformation, which always leads to behavioral change.

So I asked Jayne, "What are you believing about yourself now?"

"I'm loved. I'm not alone—God is with me. I'm not powerless because I am more than a conqueror through him."

"And what are you experiencing?" I asked as I pointed to the top of the tree. As Jayne spoke, I wrote down the new fruit she said she was experiencing: "Love, joy, peace, and hope."[2]

We are not saved just once in our past. We continue being saved in the present. God's salvation didn't just happen to us. It is also continuing to happen. He is actively saving us. The gospel is good news for our sanctification—the ongoing work

---

2. One of the reasons I could lead Jayne through this process the way I did is that she knows the gospel and she knows the Bible well. In order for you to guide someone through a process like this, that person needs to be familiar with the gospel and the truths found in the Scriptures. For those who don't yet know the truths of the gospel, we need to share what we know to be true about Jesus. In other words, we need to give them the gospel vocabulary first.

of God saving us and conforming us daily into the image of Christ. Our activity in this process is ongoing repentance from unbelief to belief in the gospel.

Paul said that as we repent and believe the gospel—as we turn to, look at, and believe in Jesus—we are transformed, increasingly becoming more and more like Jesus: "And we all, with unveiled face, beholding the glory of the Lord, are being transformed into the same image from one degree of glory to another. For this comes from the Lord who is the Spirit" (2 Cor. 3:18).

I encourage you to begin paying close attention to the fruit of your life, but don't make the mistake of engaging in a self-change project. With the help of the Spirit, and ideally in community with others who love Jesus and believe the gospel, practice tracing the fruit to the root. Examine what you have been believing and where your beliefs are not in line with the truth of the gospel. Confess what you believe out loud. What is the sin under the sins? What sinful beliefs have you been holding?

Once you trace the fruit to the root, invite the Spirit to reveal the truth of who God is and what he has done for you in Christ. Ask him to give you the ability to see and believe the truth, repent from lies or unbelief, and turn to God in faith through Jesus. In other words, work your way from root to fruit. This work requires knowing the gospel and spending regular time reading the Bible so as to be more equipped to speak the truth of God to the circumstances or situations you find yourself or others in.

If you begin to do this more often, you will find yourself being transformed more and more into the image of Jesus Christ. As a result, you will also become more and more fluent in the gospel, because the more you are changed by the gospel, the more you will want to talk about it. We all talk about what most affects us. And as you do, you and others will become more fluent together.

But remember, you can't do this alone. You're weren't meant to. You need to be immersed in a gospel-fluent community.

So let's consider how to grow in gospel fluency through immersion in such a community.

PART 4

THE GOSPEL WITH US

10

EATING TO REMEMBER

In chapter 3 of this book, I described how we learn a language through immersion. I learned Spanish because I was surrounded by people speaking it constantly. The family I lived with didn't speak English, and the people in the places where I hung out didn't speak it well. So I was immersed in Spanish constantly. By contrast, several of my classmates lived in homes where the families spoke English very well. As a result, they didn't learn Spanish as quickly because they didn't have to. They weren't fully immersed in it every day.

If you and others around you are going to grow in gospel fluency, you need consistent immersion in a gospel-speaking community. This needs to be much more than a weekly gathering of the church where the gospel is preached (though it should include this). It also should be more than a weekly Bible study, small-group gathering, or missional-community meeting (though I also recommend these). Growth in gospel fluency requires regularly being with others who know and love Jesus, speak about him often, and commit together to regularly remind one another of the gospel when they forget.

In my first book, I described how to engage the everyday rhythms of life as disciple-making opportunities. I showed how we can engage in eating, listening, celebrating, blessing, resting, and working intentionally on mission. I want to revisit some of those rhythms to discover how they can help us grow in gospel fluency. We will look at celebrating through eating in this chapter, then consider listening and blessing through showing and telling in chapters 13 and 14.[1]

Remembering through Eating

From the very beginning of the story, the act of eating has played a very significant role in the worship and remembrance of who God is, what he has done, and who we are. God provided a great place for Adam and Eve to live, with all the food they needed. They regularly had the opportunity to remember God, his word, and his work, as well as who they were and what they were called to do. For them, every meal was a time to remember God's abundant provision and express their worship of him alone.

God loves us and takes care of our daily needs in generously creative ways. Think about it: he gave us five senses with which to enjoy every meal. He could have made us like an electric

---

1. Story is one of the other rhythms, one that we address in chapter 4 and other sections of this book. Re-creating—resting and working—is addressed indirectly in a few places as well. For more on all these rhythms, go to https://saturatetheworld.com /everyday-rhythms, or see chapter 15, "Everyday Rhythms," in *Saturate: Being Disciples of Jesus in the Everyday Stuff of Life* (Wheaton, IL: Crossway, 2015).

car—plug in a few times a day and get energy to keep going. But he didn't. He wants us to enjoy eating for his glory.

When we eat, we see that our food looks good. Some meals look like a painting by Monet, others look like a Picasso, but they are all works of art. We can smell our food. Just think of all the wonderful aromas of the best meals you've had. Don't you love them! And as you put your food in your mouth, there's an explosion of sensations—sweet, sour, bitter, salty.[2] It's like a party in your mouth! And you don't just taste your food, you feel it as well. There are so many textures to experience. And then you hear it as it crunches, sloshes, or slurps its way into your body (some people are annoyed at this part of eating). Through all of this, you are nourished and replenished, strengthened and rebuilt.

God wants us to eat and remember—to enjoy and worship him—and, at the same time, have our needs met by him.

Remember what he said to Adam and Eve: "Eat from any tree in the garden except the tree of the knowledge of good and evil. If you eat of that tree, you will surely die" (see Gen. 2:16–17). Every meal was an opportunity to remember, trust, and obey. Every meal was meant to be an act of remembrance and worship.

But they did not remember, trust, and obey. They ate unto themselves.

God designed them to trust in his ability to provide for them. Something outside of them was meant to take care of a deep need inside of them—and he would provide that something. They were not to look outside of his provision.

All of this was meant to point us toward God's ultimate

---

2. Along with these four, umami (pleasant savory taste) was added to the list of basic tastes in 1985, and studies are showing that there may be seven or more additional tastes that the mouth is capable of distinguishing: calcium, kokumi, piquance, coolness, metallicity, fat, and carbon dioxide. God has given us a complex sense of taste so we can enjoy everything that he has given us to eat in this world.

provision in Jesus. Eventually, Jesus came to be God's ultimate provision for us. He is the bread of life that meets our deepest needs and satisfies our greatest longings. Every meal is meant to cause us to remember and worship Jesus.

Everyday Meals

What if your friends, your family, your small group, or your missional community made it a point to make every single meal a remembrance and worship experience? What if you slowed down enough to remember Jesus at every meal? What if you savored every moment as an opportunity to praise God?

I love eating meals with Aaron Spiro! Aaron is a member of Soma Tacoma, my former church, and a quintessential worship leader. He makes everything worshipful. That's why he is especially great to eat with.

At one especially memorable meal, it was all "mmms" and "ahhs" from his side of the table. "This steak is so *good*!" he exclaimed. "Perfectly cooked. It tastes amazing! We praise you, Jesus, for this incredible food! And look at it all. Isn't everything so beautiful. Look at the colors, the creativity, the beauty of it all." He then lifted a glass: "Praise the root of Jesse! Not only has he blessed us with a fruitful harvest, but he also has given us abundance in this wine. Thank you, Father, for all your good gifts to us and thank you especially for Jesus!"

At one point, he got so carried away that he said: "This food is so good, eating it is like a religious experience. I don't want anything to come between this food and me. It should be as if we're in the garden again—naked and unashamed. I just want to rip off my shirt and eat." At that point, we knew he'd gone too far. He's a hairy man, so we requested that he keep his shirt on!

What if we worshiped Jesus at every meal like that (well, except for the last part)? Not every meal needs to be an elaborate feast, though I recommend you have those once in a while. However, what if you took time at every meal—even very simple ones—to give thanks to God, praying not just at the beginning, but throughout the meal?

Every time I pray at the beginning of a meal, I take time to remember Jesus as the better provision. And I usually pray in such a way as to set up the meal as a time of worshiping Jesus together. Sometimes we intentionally use the mealtime to rehearse the evidences of God's grace to us. Since we're already in the posture of receiving when we eat, why not take time to reflect on all the other ways we've received his grace?

Our family is trying to use our evening mealtimes more intentionally. We are presently rehearsing the Ten Commandments and going through the gospel with each one of them.

We also have given each night a theme to guide what we do together at the meal. On *Mission Monday*, we remember together our family's mission to glorify God and fulfill his purposes in saving us. We take time to discuss how our week needs to be ordered in light of our family's mission and our missional community's mission. One Monday night, we were discussing some close friends of ours who were financially struggling because of the cost of adopting two Ethiopian children. We together agreed that we should pay for their rent the next month. So we talked through how the gospel informs giving, and our children, who were thirteen, eleven, and nine at the time, together came up with a third of the amount we would end up giving. We also discussed how we would cut some spending as a family to care for our friends' need.

Teaching Tuesday is when one of the children takes responsibility for our learning from God's word at the meal. I want them to learn how to lead a Bible discussion and ask gospel-centered questions. Parents, it's our responsibility to raise up gospel-fluent children who know their Bibles, can find the truths of Jesus within their Bibles, and can speak those truths faithfully to others in need of the gospel.

With-Family Wednesday is the night when we eat with our missional community. Our time together around the meal is always a great experience of remembrance. Sometimes we more specifically remember Jesus's life, death, and resurrection by formally breaking bread and drinking from the cup.

Thanksgiving Thursday is when we take time to give thanks for all God has done. We also put a person on the "hot seat" and express why we are thankful to God for him or her. I love it when we have a visitor with us, as it is a great opportunity for us to bless another person with words. My kids always request that we put the visitor on the hot seat on these nights. They're learning to think of others as more important than themselves because this is how Jesus thought of us (Phil. 2:1–11).

On *Fun Friday*, we go out to eat, or we eat together and then go to a movie, have a game night, or take a special outing. Gospel remembrance happens through enjoying a good meal and a movie, then discussing what in the movie was in line with the gospel and what wasn't. I've found that talking through a movie together is a great way to train our eyes and ears toward gospel sensitivity. Playing a game also provides plenty of gospel opportunities as we work through our responses to winning and losing in light of the gospel.

Serving Saturday often means we are with others for a meal or serving some people. And Sunday is when we remember Jesus through taking communion together at our church's gathering. This is another way to remember through a meal—*the* meal, the Lord's Supper.

The Meal

On the night Jesus was betrayed, he shared the Passover meal with his disciples. That meal commemorated the night when

God struck down every firstborn son of Egypt while protecting his people from the same fate. Their protection came through the Passover lambs that were sacrificed and eaten inside homes where the doorposts had been covered with the lambs' blood. This was the final straw for Pharaoh, and he finally let God's people go. Ever after, the Passover was a remembrance meal of God's redemption of Israel out of slavery.

At his last meal with his disciples before his death, Jesus showed how every Passover meal had pointed to him. And at this meal, Jesus changed the Passover to the Lord's Supper as his meal. It became a meal at which we remember how he redeemed us out of slavery to sin and Satan by becoming the true and better sacrificial Lamb of God for us.

Jesus picked up the bread, and when he had given thanks, he broke it and gave it to them, saying: "This is my body, which is given for you. Do this in remembrance of me." And he took a cup, and when he had given thanks, he gave it to them, and they all drank of it. And he said to them, "This is my blood of the covenant, which is poured out for many."[3]

The church where I presently serve remembers Jesus's death every Sunday in our music, in our preaching, and through the meal. In our desire to see our people grow in gospel fluency, we made space in our schedule, as well as in our facility, for them to take the bread and cup together in a meaningful way. We usually set up our time of remembrance following the preaching of a gospel-centered message. We encourage people to go and pick up some bread, dip it in the cup, and get into a circle with their friends, family members, or missional-community members. We encourage them to speak the gospel to one another through the elements, often in light of the message they have just heard. For example, when I taught on the importance of silence and solitude, people took the bread and reminded

---

3. This is a harmony of the accounts from Mark 14:22–24 and Luke 22:17–20.

one other that in his body, Jesus was all alone on the cross and was silent before his accusers. His blood (the cup) was shed for us so that we can sit in silence and not hear a condemning word spoken over us. Instead, we hear words of loving acceptance from our heavenly Father. In this way, our people get to practice sharing the gospel with one another in a variety of ways every week and then grow in praying it together as well.

Paul said, "For as often as you eat this bread and drink the cup, you proclaim the Lord's death until he comes" (1 Cor. 11:26). We should remember Jesus regularly with *the* meal and practice proclaiming his death to one another through it.

Good News to One Another

Another helpful practice for both remembrance and growth in gospel proclamation is to speak the gospel through the elements to one another's needs, hurts, and longings in small-group gatherings or missional-community meetings.

I first tried this during a missional-community gathering at our home in January several years ago. I explained to our group that I wanted each of them to share something they were struggling with; a desire they had that was yet to be met; or doubts or fears they might be experiencing. Then one of us would take the bread and the cup, and speak the truths of Jesus's body given and blood shed for us to the need.

I volunteered to start.

I shared: "I'm pretty discouraged right now. This past year was not what I had hoped. I feel as if our church wasn't as fruitful this year as I wanted. I'm discouraged about my leadership and some ways in which I believe I've failed."

Randy jumped forward, grabbed the bread and cup, and began to encourage and exhort me: "Jeff, I want to remind you that you don't build the church. Jesus does. And your righteousness is not based on your own performance, but on Jesus's performance for you. It doesn't matter how well or how poorly you did."

Then, as he held up first the bread and then the cup, he went on to say: "Jesus's life was given for you. His body of righteousness was sacrificed for you. And he shed his blood for you. Every sin you've committed, every way in which you fell short, was paid for. You are forgiven for making this about you and making it dependent on you. Receive his body and blood for you. Receive his grace!"

I took the bread and cup, ate and drank, and remembered. It was good news to me!

Then Nikki spoke up: "You kids are all so young. Look at you! Here you are at the beginning of your adult lives and you know Jesus. It took me until I was in my seventies to finally come to Jesus. I don't know why it took me so long. I have so many regrets. So many things I wish were different. Don't waste your lives! You have your whole life to live for Jesus. I have so little left."

One of the women grabbed the bread and the cup, then began to address Nikki: "Nikki, it is true. We have many more years to love and serve Jesus. It is true that you spent most of your life without him. But you can be certain he was there. And he is the Redeemer. He's *your* Redeemer. He takes the years that you believe you wasted and redeems them all back as though none of them is gone. He replenishes what was lost with his own life.

"You have the righteousness of Christ," she said, holding up the bread, "in exchange for your life of sin. He bought all the wasted years back for you with his life and death. And besides, your life is a testimony, a story of his grace. And he poured out his blood," she added, holding up the cup, "for the forgiveness of your sins. No more regrets, Nikki! No more. You are forgiven and cleansed from all your sin."

Nikki's eyes were full of tears as she broke off a piece of the bread and ate it, then drank from the cup.

We continued around the circle: one after another, we confessed our need for a Savior, and one after another, we proclaimed the good news of Jesus to our very real needs. It was an incredibly joyous and tear-filled experience of grace!

I've led this same experience many times with brand-new Christians as well as church leaders. It isn't always the same experience. Some people are not very fluent in the gospel and therefore struggle with how to speak it to specific needs. However, I let people know that's OK when I start and that those in the group will help one another. I usually ask for someone to volunteer to share, and let the person to the right know he or she will be asked to speak the gospel to the need. I then say: "If you don't know what to say, let us know and the rest of us will help. Over time, we will all get better at this."

God has given us many ways to remember him and grow in proclaiming the gospel. They are around us all the time in what is called general revelation—creation and the rhythms of life within it. Our job is to learn to see the truths of God in the everyday life around us and speak the truths of the gospel into it.

The meal—"the Jesus Supper"—is the one he told us to use to regularly remember him. It is also one of the most effective ways I have found to train us to do this in all the other places of life as well.

Start with *the* meal every week, then practice remembering Jesus at the other meals, and you will have twenty-two[4] stops through your week in gospel remembrance and proclamation.

If you do this, you will be well on your way to growing in gospel fluency with others!

---

4. Three meals a day, seven days a week, is twenty-one meals. Then add *the* meal—"the Jesus Supper"—and you have twenty-two.

11

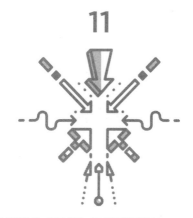

HE'S THE BETTER . . .

"I can't stand my job! I've been working there for too long to be treated like this," she said.

We had just started eating dinner at our weekly missional community family meal when one of our members started unloading her frustrations about work. "I should have received a raise a long time ago and I am still in the same position that I started in two years ago," she went on to say. "My boss keeps telling me I will eventually get a promotion, but it seems as if I keep getting overlooked. I'm really tired of this! I'm ready to quit."

She continued sharing her frustrations about the working conditions and the poor benefits, and how her coworkers didn't help the situation, because most of them had bad attitudes and poor work ethics.

This kind of conversation is fairly normal for group life in a church—and for life in community anywhere, for that matter. We struggle with work and want a place to vent. Likewise, we experience pain and frustration in our relationships. Roommates get on our nerves. Finances are not always abundant or predictable. Parents wound us or let us down. So do children. We have plenty to talk about and often much to complain about.

At times like these, we need to remind ourselves and one another that Jesus is better.

The Better Boss

Typically, in a gathering like this, the initial response to our sister's complaints is additional complaining:

"I know what you mean! My job stinks as well."

"You deserve better! Your boss doesn't know what he has in you. Maybe one day he'll wake up and realize what an incredible person you are!"

"Yeah, well, it might be too late when he does, because if I were you, I'd quit!"

A gospel community can do better than that.

A community committed to growing in gospel fluency together doesn't respond like everyone else. We have good news to bring to bear on the difficulties of life. Sure, it's good to enter into someone's pain and struggle with empathy. However, we also have good news to give.

I regularly encourage our groups to ask these questions: (1) How does the gospel bring good news to this situation? (2) What about the gospel do we need to hear right now? (3) What about the gospel have we forgotten or failed to believe? and (4) How is Jesus better than what we have or what we want?

"You're forgetting the gospel," another of our group members chimed in. "You're forgetting what is true for you because of Jesus."

I was so encouraged when I heard this! "I think we're starting to grow in gospel fluency," I thought.

She continued: "I know you might believe you deserve better pay. You are a good worker at your job. But I want to remind you of what we all deserve apart from Jesus's death on our behalf. We deserve death."

When she said this, I remembered times when my children, while riding in our minivan in climate-controlled comfort while sitting in reclining leather captain's seats and watching a DVD on the drop-down video screen, would give in to complaints.

"I don't like this movie!"

"She's too close to me!"

"I'm too hot."

"I'm too cold, roll up the window!"

At these times, I would often stop the minivan and ask them a question: "What do you all deserve?"

"Death," they would respond in unison.

"That's right," I would say. "Because of our sin, we deserve death, but because of Jesus's death, we get to live not just today, but forever. You're alive! Thank God for Jesus! Thank God for your life. Are you guys thankful?"

"Yes," they would generally reply, while still mumbling less discernible complaints under their breath.

You might think I'm a bit extreme. Maybe.

But it is true—we don't deserve what we have. We are so blessed! And it's amazing how easy it is to complain when we forget what we really deserve. It's also much easier to give thanks when we remember what we've received in comparison.

I've found that gospel thankfulness is a great cure for complaining.

The woman in our group continued: "You deserve death and hell, but God has given you eternal life through Jesus Christ our Lord. You're getting far better than you deserve!"

"And don't forget the promotion you've already received," someone else chimed in. "You were imprisoned and enslaved under the rule of the Devil, and Jesus not only redeemed and delivered you out of slavery to sin, but through him you have been seated with Christ in the heavenly realms (Eph. 2:6). Talk about a promotion!"

"And that's not all," another member spoke up, "Your boss may not recognize the work you're doing. He might not build you up much with his words, but Jesus is presently speaking far better words about you before God the Father. Sure, it's great to get your boss's approval, but you don't have to have it because the God of the universe, who created your boss, is giving you his approval in Christ."

"And remember," the young woman who started us in this direction said, "you have an incredible benefits package."

It was actually fun coming up with all the ways life in Christ is better.

"You have been blessed with every spiritual blessing in the heavenly places and will enjoy a new heaven and earth forever, where there will be no more sickness or death, suffering or brokenness," I added. "You have it better than you think. Don't forget how good you have it in Jesus Christ. And remember, your company's boss is not your real boss. Jesus is. Go to work for Jesus tomorrow. Work for him with all your heart as an act of worship. He deserves it!"

Jesus is the better boss!

A Better Son Showing a Better Father

Part of our job as a gospel-fluent community is to continue to remind one another that Jesus is "the better." He is the better boss. He is also the better worker, who did a far better job than us. He is the better friend, who died for us. He is the better Son, who perfectly obeyed the Father on our behalf—and on our children's behalf as well.

Parents, some of you need to remember this. Your children fail. They're not perfect. And they were not meant to live the life you thought you should have. Many parents are trying to live vicariously through their children, silently saying to them: "Be the athlete I wish I had been. Get the grades I could never earn. Gain the popularity I could never attain. Give me the relationship I never had with my parents."

So many parents see their children as substitutes for their childhood. But children can't handle this weight. It will crush them. And that will disappoint parents who think this way.

There is only one perfect child. Jesus is the better child.

Your children need to know and believe this. You do as well.

Maybe you're not the parent. Maybe you're the child who needs to know that Jesus is better. I found that my brother Jerry was one of those children. He needed Jesus to be the better son for him.

I remember a powerful conversation I had with him a few years back. He had just stepped into the company that my father had started the year I was born. It had a good reputation in our hometown and had been successful for many years. However, the business was not doing as well as it had; in fact, it was taking a fast nosedive. So Dad had asked Jerry to step in and try to save it (which he eventually did).

One day, Jerry and I were talking about how the business was doing, and while we talked, I could tell he was discouraged. Business was getting better, but he wasn't. As I prodded a bit, I realized that his biggest problem wasn't the success of the business. His problem was that he didn't feel that Dad was proud of him. He wanted our father's approval.

We all want this, don't we? We want our parents to be proud of us.

Well, the truth is, our dad was incredibly proud of Jerry. I knew that because my parents regularly spoke about how proud they were of him. It occurred to me then that Jerry wanted to be the perfect son, one who accomplished perfect work and received perfect approval from a perfect dad. But none of this would happen if he continued to look to himself and to our earthly father for it.

"Jerry, you're looking in the wrong place," I said. "It sounds like, if you were convinced that Dad was proud of you and that your work was great, then you would feel better. The problem is that you are looking to Dad to provide something for you that only God can provide perfectly. You want to do well and you want approval. Those are not bad things. But you're looking to the wrong source. Because Dad is imperfect, his approval of you will always be imperfect. And because you are imperfect, you will always know that you can do better.

"Jerry, you need to repent of expecting Dad to be God for you. He will fail to give you the approval you really need. No matter how many times he tells you how much he is proud of you, it will always come up a little short. This is because he is just as in need of approval from God as you are.

"Can I encourage you to stop looking at Dad as your true Father? We have a good dad, but he's not a perfect dad. Only God the Father is. Let Dad be more like a brother to you. Let him be in need of our heavenly Father's approval just as you are. And then, let him off the hook for failing to be perfect. There's only one perfect Father, and Dad is not him. And let yourself off the hook as well. You don't have to be the perfect son either. In fact, you can't be. Jesus is that for you. Jesus both shows you who your true Father is and grants you the Father's approval because of his performance on your behalf."

That was the first of many similar conversations that Jerry and I have had over the past several years. I've watched the gospel grip his heart more and more. And the more it has, the more joy-filled he has become.

Jesus shows us the better Father and is for us the better Son.

The Four Questions

This is what we need to practice doing together in our groups. We need to keep pointing one another to Jesus and showing how he is the better everything.

How do we do this?

First, as a reminder, it is important to establish the group in the four key questions that we walked through in chapter 9: (1) Who is God/Jesus? (2) What has he done or what is he doing? (3) Who are we in light of that work? and (4) How should we live in light of who we are?

Let's think about how these questions might have been answered in regard to the young woman with an unlikable job and bad boss. (1) Who is God/Jesus? Jesus is her Lord, her boss. And he is a good, great, gracious, and generous boss! (2) What has he done for her (in other words, how do we know he is a good boss)? He did not come to be served but to serve and give his life as her ransom. He didn't give her the wages she deserves. The wages of sin is death, but the gift of God is eternal life through Jesus Christ our Lord (the better boss). And he sat down at the right hand of God the Father, where he is making constant intercession (speaking great words on her behalf) with the Father for her. (3) Who is she in light of that work? She is seated with him in the heavenly realms, a child of God, approved of by the Father, a beneficiary of all that belongs to Jesus, and she now serves as an ambassador for the King of kings. (4) How should she live? She should work with joy, freedom, power, and hope.

We go to work for Jesus, the only boss worthy of our worship, deserving of our thanks, and capable of granting us genuine, lasting approval.

You could try the same exercise with any situation or struggle. As a matter of practice, pick a relationship or situation (spouse, friend, child, work, provision, identity) and work through these questions together as a group.

Get to Know the Overall Story

Another way to grow in seeing Jesus as the better is to get to know the larger story of the Bible. I walked through a condensed version of it in chapter 4.

So many people read the Bible as a bunch of individual stories. Sure, there are plenty of stories in the Bible, but the point of the whole Bible is to tell the one true story—the true and better story of the world. It is the story of God and his redeeming love. It is the story of his pursuit of us to rescue and restore us to relationships with him, one another, and a renewed creation.

In one sense, the whole Bible is the gospel—the good news that God has come to rescue and restore humanity and all creation in and through the person and work of Jesus Christ. And every part of the Bible either points forward or backward to Jesus because he is the heart—the center—of the story. The entire Bible also shows how desperately needy every single person is for God's salvation.

Jesus is the point of every story, the fulfillment of every longing, the completion of everything that is lacking. Every character, story, and theme points to him because the whole story is about him.

So how can you learn to read the Bible this way?

I recommend you go through the story of God together as a group regularly.[1] There are many ways to do this. New Tribes

---

1. It's especially helpful to have people who don't yet believe in Jesus go through it as well. We often miss much because we assume we've asked every question. But people new to the Bible awaken us to many new questions, thoughts, and perspectives because they hear it with different ears and see it with fresh eyes.

Mission developed a way to tell the whole biblical story years ago.[2] The International Mission Board of the Southern Baptist Convention also has developed many story sets to teach people the gospel where there is no Bible in written form.[3] The leadership of Soma Tacoma developed *The Story of God* as a key discipleship tool for our church. Following that, we developed a condensed version of the same material, *The Story-Formed Way*.[4] Many other great resources have come out since. Parents, a great tool to use with your children is *The Jesus Storybook Bible* by Sally Lloyd-Jones (ZonderKidz, 2007).

I am increasingly convinced and concerned that most Christians can't tell the whole story of the Bible. Therefore, they likely can't show how it all leads to Jesus as the better. I encourage you to take advantage of some of the helpful resources that are available to learn the story thoroughly.

Read the Whole Bible

I also strongly encourage you to commit to regularly reading through your Bible—the whole thing. So many Christians have never read their Bibles. Sure, they have favorite sections they read over and over again, but they haven't read the entire book. As a result, most don't know the whole story, so they often wrongly interpret Scripture out of context. When you don't know the whole story of God, you tend toward making the Bible about you and not about Jesus.

I made it my goal years ago to read through my Bible once every year. Sometimes I read it from cover to cover. Other times, I read it using a chronological reading plan. I've used Robert Murray McCheyne's reading plan. I even read through *The*

---

2. *Creation to Christ* adult chronological Bible study, http://www.ntmbookstore.com/chronological-bible-study-s/2033.htm.

3. See https://orality.imb.org/resources/?t=13.

4. See *The Story-Formed Way*, https://saturatetheworld.com/story-formed-way/; *The Story of God*, https://saturatetheworld.com/story-of-god; and *The Story of God for Kids*, https://saturatetheworld.com/story-of-god-for-kids.

Message, Eugene Peterson's unique translation of the Bible, as my reading plan one year. The more I read, the more I get to know the whole story. And the more I see the whole story, the more I see Christ throughout the story.

I highly recommend that you commit with others to do this. I have found that people are more successful in reading through the entire Bible when they do it with others in their small group or missional community. This allows them to learn together and hold one another accountable for their reading.

Find Jesus in the Story

As you get to know your Bible, look to see Jesus in every text by looking for the typology of Jesus in every story or situation. The Bible is not just recounting the story as it occurred, but in such a way as to create an anticipation, a longing, for a better person, a better solution, a better fulfillment—a better Savior.

In his providence and through the inspiration of the Holy Spirit, God ensured the Scriptures would include numerous "types" (prefigurings) of Christ and would create a vacuum of longing for him to arrive and fulfill our greatest need. Learn to read the Bible, both alone and in community, while asking these questions: (1) How is this person or situation a type of Christ? (2) What is lacking in this story that only Jesus can fulfill? and (3) What is the longing or the hunger that is created here for Jesus to satisfy?

For example, Adam is a type of Christ in that he was the first human given authority over the world on behalf of God. From his sleeping body there came into existence a bride who was called to rule with him. His hour of temptation happened in the garden, yet he failed to overcome the temptation and sinned. So we have a type and longing for a better Adam.

Jesus is the firstborn of the new creation, who overcame the temptation of the Devil at the beginning of his ministry, showed his power over sin and Satan in his ministry, and then, in the garden of Gethsemane, submitted himself to God to drink the cup of suffering on the cross for the sins of Adam and his off-spring. As a result, Jesus went to "sleep" (died) and was laid to rest in a tomb, only to be raised up by God on the third day. And it was through his body that the church was brought into existence. Now he is head of the church, the new humanity, instead of sinful Adam.

We can and need to look for Jesus in every single story throughout the entire biblical narrative. Learn to do this with your family members, roommates, or those in your small group or missional community.[5]

The True and Better

Tim Keller, who has been hugely influential on my gospel fluency development, provides a concise example of this:

Jesus is the true and better Adam, who passed the test in the garden. His garden is a much tougher garden and his obedience is imputed to us.

Jesus is the true and better Abel, who, though innocently slain, has blood that cries out, not for our condemnation but for our acquittal.

Jesus is the true and better Abraham, who answers the call of God, who leaves all the familiar comforts of the world [to go] into the void, not knowing where he went.

Jesus is the true and better Isaac, who is not only offered by his father on the mount but who was truly sacrificed for us all. While God said to Abraham, "Now I know you truly love me, because you did not withhold your son, your only son, from me," now we, at the foot of the cross, can say to

---

5. Tim Keller's preaching is some of the best I've heard at bringing us to Jesus through every text. Edmund Clowney's books and teaching are also helpful tools; you may want to do a group study through one of his books, such as *The Unfolding Mystery: Discovering Christ in the Old Testament*, 2nd ed. (Phillipsburg, NJ: P&R, 2013).

God, "Now we know you love us because you did not with-hold your Son, your only Son, whom you love, from us."

Jesus is the true and better Jacob, who wrestled and took the blows of justice we deserve so we, like Jacob, only receive the wounds of grace that wake us up and disciple us.

Jesus is the true and better Joseph, who is at the right hand of the king, and forgives those who betrayed and sold him and uses his power to save them.

Jesus is the true and better Moses, who stands in the gap between the people and the Lord and mediates the new covenant.

Jesus is the true and better rock of Moses, who, struck with the rod of God's justice, now gives us water in the desert.

Jesus is the true and better Job, the truly innocent suf-ferer who then intercedes for and saves his stupid friends.

Jesus is the true and better David, whose victory be-comes the people's victory though they didn't lift a stone to accomplish it themselves.

Jesus is the true and better Esther, who didn't just risk losing an earthly palace but lost ultimately the heavenly one, who didn't just risk his life but gave his life, who didn't say, "If I perish, I perish," but, "When I perish, I will perish for them . . . to save my people."

Jesus is the true and better Jonah, who was cast out into the storm so we could be brought in. He's the real Passover Lamb; he's the true temple, the true prophet, the true priest, the true king, the true sacrifice, the true lamb, the true light, the true bread.[6]

Jesus is better.
Jesus is *the* better.

---

6. Tim Keller, "Excerpts from a Sermon: *Gospel-Centered Ministry, 1 Peter 1:1–12 and 1:22-2:12*," available online at https://issuu.com/gospeldelta/docs/tim-keller-gospel-centered-ministry/6.

He is the better Adam, the better Noah, the better Abraham, and the better Moses.

He is the better ark, the better manna, the better water, and the better wine.

He is the better temple, the better priest, and the better sacrifice. He's the better spouse, the better parent, the better son, and the better boss.

Don't settle for substitutes. Don't try to be a substitute. Jesus did better than anyone or anything. Jesus does better than anyone or anything. And Jesus will do better than anyone or anything.

Jesus is the better *everything*!

Don't look elsewhere and don't give one another anything or anyone else. Remind one another of the truths about Jesus in a gospel-fluent community. And be reminded yourself as you submit to others speaking into your life and experience that Jesus is the better.

Give one another Jesus. He's better.

12

THE HERO OF OUR STORY

In chapter 4, I shared that our personal stories shape how we understand our world and language. Story is also how we shape culture. Listening to one another's stories enables us to learn about God's work in one another as well. Every one of us has a story, and all of our stories are part of the true story. Really, our story is God's story. Though we regularly believe they are about us, our stories are really all about him, for "in him we live and move and have our being" (Acts 17:28).

Brian Godawa, an award-winning filmmaker, has put it well:

We are creatures of story, created by a storytelling God, who created the very fabric of our reality in terms of his story. Rather than seeing our existence as a series of unconnected random events without purpose, storytelling brings meaning to our lives through the analogy of carefully crafted plot that reflects the loving sovereignty of the God of the Bible.[1]

When I begin a new missional community, one of the first things I have the members do is share their stories. I have found that you can discover a lot about people's beliefs and their gospel fluency from the way they tell their stories. One of the key questions I ask as I listen to someone tell his or her story is this: "Who is the hero of this story?"

If you're into film or good fiction, as I am, you can generally discover the hero of a story fairly quickly. The hero generally is brought into the narrative early, with a significant amount of character development designed to draw you in, build your interest in this person, and win you over to her. Some writers like to keep the hero hidden to create a sense of longing and intrigue, but there still is no doubt by the end who the hero of the story is. The hero stands out above everyone else.

As I listen to many Christians share their stories, I often find that Jesus has become a supporting character, not the hero.

Often, a person spends large chunks of time describing his life before meeting Jesus, going into more detail about his sin than anyone needs to know. Jesus is just a small blip on the radar: "I realized I needed to be forgiven of my sins, and Joe introduced me to Jesus and how he died on the cross for me, so I asked him into my heart." Then the person goes on to share how hard he has tried to be a better person, but he fails a lot. For instance, he is going to church more often and trying to read his Bible and pray, but life is busy. "Thank God he forgives us!"

By the end of the story, you have heard a lot of sin, self, and self-effort, but very little Jesus and very little good news.

---

1. Brian Godawa, *Hollywood Worldviews: Watching Films with Wisdom & Discernment* (Downers Grove, IL: IVP, 2011), 71.

Often, as in my illustration, the emphasis is on a decision the person made or a welcoming invitation he extended to Jesus. Unfortunately, the person telling the story is the hero.

By the way, Jesus doesn't wait for invitations into our hearts. He comes to rescue us from our slavery to sin and Satan. He invades enemy territory, breaks through the stone walls of our hearts, and delivers us from death!

He's the hero, not us.

Sometimes when I have people share their stories, Jesus is not a part of them at all. You might hear about church or religious practices, but nothing about Jesus. You might be surprised by how many so-called "Christians" have little to no Jesus in their stories.

Now, to be clear, when this happens, I don't shame people or come down hard on them. I actually do this exercise in order to hear what people really believe. The point isn't grading people on how fluent in the gospel they are. The point is loving one another enough to hear what people believe and to be ready to lead them gently to initial faith or growing faith in Jesus.

Remember, it is out of the overflow of the heart that the mouth speaks. You talk most about what you love most. My goal in leading a group toward gospel fluency is, first of all, to find out if they know and believe the gospel. If they do, I then want to discover how much their faith in Jesus is shaping their lives. If there is little to no Jesus in their stories, then we need to lay a gospel foundation and pray God grants them genuine faith in Jesus.

Ways to Tell the Story

I use a variety of methods to have people share their stories.

Recently, I used a method called "Instagram Stories." I gave each group member a poster-sized Post-it note and a set of markers. I then instructed each person to draw twelve equal-sized boxes on it. Each box was to represent a different part of his or her story. And for each part of the story, I asked each group member to draw a still-frame picture that captured the essence of that stage. After they finished drawing, I asked them to talk us through their stories using the pictures. This is a great way for people who are visual learners to engage. It also helps those who get nervous speaking in front of people by providing an opportunity for them to focus on the pictures while sharing their stories.

I've also told people to tell their stories using three key events as pillars to build on. For instance, in my story, the first pillar is the shame that I experienced as a seventh grader, when our pastor publicly embarrassed me in front of fifty or more junior high and high school students. That continued into high school, as I observed teenagers who became pregnant brought in front of the congregation to highlight what they had done. Unfortunately, since I knew only the good news that Jesus "saves us from hell," I didn't know he can also remove our shame in the present. As a result, I looked to myself to deal with shame instead of Jesus. But the only way you can deal with shame apart from Jesus is to perform better and hide more. I tried both. I worked harder at sports, music, and popularity, while I also found more sophisticated ways to hide my sin. I increased my efforts, but my shame just piled up more and more as I went further into hiding. I didn't run to Jesus for help. I ran from him and everyone else for fear of being found out. I learned how to lead a double life.

My next pillar is the day when Jesus revealed his love and grace to me while I was in Denia, Spain. In the midst of my sin and shame, he showed up and invited me to surrender my life to him. He revealed to me through the gospel that he knew everything I had done and forgave me for all of it. I knew my guilt was atoned for and my sin was taken away. He saved me and set me free. When I tell my story, I share how Jesus continued to lead me as I learned to follow him through a growing dependence upon him daily.

Eventually, I get to my third pillar, the time when my people-pleasing idol was revealed in a very painful period of my life. I couldn't keep everyone happy and also do what was right. I was caught, and it led to a time of significant depression. I discovered that it was the loving discipline of our heavenly Father that had brought me to that point. Clearly, I had been saved that day in Spain. However, God wasn't finished with me. He was still saving me. It was during this time that I came to see that Jesus is more powerful than the opinion of man and that, in Jesus, I had received the approval of God my Father, whose approval matters more than anyone else's.

Three pillars, three key events. Jesus is the hero in all three.

Over the years, I've grown in telling my story—his story—so that I am the supporting character, not the main character. This change is part of growing in gospel fluency.

A third way that we've helped people grow in making Jesus the hero of their stories is by using the four movements of the one true story to help them frame their own stories: Creation, Fall, Redemption, and New Creation.

Creation

Creation is all about identity. What do we believe about our origin and purpose? We all have fundamental beliefs about our origins—who or what gave us our existence, made us who we are, and shaped us into the people we are today. We all have learned to find our identity in someone or something.

"How did we get here?" and "Why are we here?" are the questions we are answering in this part of our stories.

The key question is, "What was my *identity* in?"

Many find their identity in their parents or other significant influencers. However, as these influencers fail them, people move on to other things, such as work, fitness, appearance, or possessions, for their sense of identity.

When I teach people how to tell their stories in light of the creation narrative, I encourage them to identify what they looked to or still tend to depend on for their sense of identity. What do they trust for their sense of worth and value?

My identity was based on people's approval of me based on my good performance, or at least my good image. Before Jesus, and even at times since I came to faith in Jesus, I didn't view myself in light of how God sees me.

I encourage people to start their stories by talking about their background, some of their early shaping influences, and how these provided a framework for their sense of identity.

Remember, the true story grounds our identity in our creation as image bearers of God, put into the world to represent what he is like in all we do. However, because of sin, we all have been born into brokenness, and the image of God in us is distorted. Also, we have been raised by broken image-bearers who have given us a distorted picture of God, self, and others.

This leads to the second movement of our story.

Fall

The fall is about brokenness. In this movement of our stories, we share what has destroyed or is destroying our identity and purpose. The world is not as it should be. We are not as we should be. Brokenness is all around us and in us. Why are things broken? How did we get broken? Who is to blame for our brokenness?

These are the kinds of questions people are dealing with in the fall movement of their stories.

The key question is, "Who or what was the *problem* in my life?"

Everyone believes in a dominant problem that is keeping them from being who they were made to be or doing what they believe they are supposed to do. Most people tend to blame someone else for what is wrong. Often, it is what their parents did or did not do to them or for them.

You will often find that when that which people look to for their sense of identity (their creation stories) fails them, that is what they blame. Sometimes their perceived problem is the culture around them or the failure of friends or coworkers. And sometimes they see themselves as the problem.

This is close to the truth, but not close enough. The problem is in us, but it isn't in how we appear or even in how we behave. It's much deeper than that. The gospel informs us that the real problem is sin—our unbelief in God. We rebelled against God and looked elsewhere for our identity, purpose, and truth, so God turned us over to our sin. And sin destroys.

As I teach people to write their stories in such as way as to make Jesus the hero, I also encourage them to take ownership of their culpability in their brokenness. We all have sinned and fallen short of the glory of God.

Identify what you have done that is broken. What have you believed about God, others, and yourself that is wrong? And how have your sinful beliefs led to sinful behaviors?

In my story, I highlight that my problem was that I looked to man for approval and acceptance. I had exchanged worship of God for seeking the approval of man.

Some people share about being abused or abandoned, physically or emotionally, as they tell their stories. All abuse is wrong. However, we need to help one another move from allowing abusers to continue to have power and control over us, making them the center of our stories, to taking ownership for how we respond to them.

Though I was not physically abused, I do believe that our pastor sinned against me by publicly shaming me. In response, I learned a coping mechanism—don't mess up (or at least don't get caught sinning) and always put on the best image possible, even if it isn't true. It would be easy to blame that pastor for my response. But that would keep me enslaved as a victim to sin, not set free from it.

When we tell our stories and fail to confess our sins, we often fail to show our need for a Savior as well. Jesus won't be the hero of the story if we don't really need a Savior for *our* sin.

So when I tell my story, I take ownership for how I responded. I came to a place where I realized that I had let others have too much power in my life. My pastor had become my image of God instead of Jesus. I had to repent of looking to my pastor and turn to Jesus. I couldn't keep blaming someone else for how I responded to God. I had to take ownership of my sin. Yes, my pastor hurt me. Yes, it was wrong. But I had sinned in looking to him to be God for me. I had rejected God to worship man—not just my pastor, but also myself.

This leads to the third movement in our stories.

Redemption

Redemption is about rescue and deliverance. Everyone is in need of a Savior. Everyone needs to be rescued and delivered. This is the part of the story where we share who or what we look to in order to save us or rescue us.

The key question is: "Who or what is our *Savior*?"

Everyone is searching for a solution to their problem. For some, it's better friends, spouses, children, or grandchildren. Some look to exercise and diets. Others believe work will save them, or the money they earn from working will do it.

Every savior, every solution, every answer, and every person falls short of addressing our real problem. Only one Savior can deal with our real problem of sin, and that is Jesus Christ.

At this point of our stories, I encourage people to share who or what they were looking to for deliverance and how they came to see that Jesus is a far better Savior, who rescued and redeemed them from sin and their slavery to it.

In my own story, I share how I idolized man and looked to others to grant me acceptance and significance. However, they always let me down. They could never say enough or do enough to address how I had sinned. I also looked to myself to try and measure up or make up the gap. I couldn't do it. In fact, it was exhausting! Only Jesus measures up for me. And only he could make up the gap of my unrighteousness with his righteous life. He paid the debt I owed for my sin and idolatry. He not only forgave me, but also healed my wounds and built me back up. Through his Spirit, he poured the love of God the Father into my heart, and as a result, I could forgive others—including my pastor.

But it doesn't end with forgiveness. The good news ends with everything being made new!

New Creation

There is a deep longing in every one of us for change, for transformation, for better—for all things to be made new. Everyone is looking forward to a final conclusion, a complete fulfillment of our every longing, a hopeful climax to every story. This is the happy ending we all long for. And this hope drives us all. We all have things in our hearts and minds that we are expectantly hoping for.

In the last part of our stories, we share what has changed in us, as well as the ultimate change we are longing for. We share how we've been transformed and what our ultimate hope is.

The key question is: "What *has changed* and what *will change*?"

We were created for more than this. What presently is is not what is to be. And every one of us longs for better, for more, for a new creation. The question is: "What is our version of the new creation?"

The gospel tells us that the new creation includes a new you, a new heaven and earth, and a new King at the center of it all—Jesus Christ. There will be a day when there will be no more sin, suffering, or brokenness. We who belong to Christ will be made perfect and complete. Heaven and earth will be new and united, and we will all worship Jesus together forever.

When I instruct people in writing their stories, I encourage them to share how Jesus has changed them and is changing them. I also encourage them to share about their hope for everything to change. The gospel is not just about what has happened. It's also good news about what is happening right now and will happen in the future. We will be saved!

God is still saving me. I am so much freer when it comes to my concern about what people think of me. I know God loves me, accepts me, and is pleased with me because of Jesus. When I fail, I am not as devastated as I used to be because I know I am forgiven and Jesus's work is sufficient. I am growing to be more like him every day, and as a result, I believe he is being more and more glorified through me, because the more I become like him, the more others get to see what he is truly like. However, I can't wait for that day to come when we will see Jesus face to face and, in a moment, become like him. The old will pass away and everything will become new! I will no longer struggle with sin. I will be made complete.

I can't wait! But I will wait and work because there are more people whom God wants to come to faith in Jesus.

Are you one of them?

Today is the day of salvation. Today is your day to respond to all Jesus has done for you. Today is the day your story can change—the day you can be changed. I urge you to recognize your need for Jesus to redeem you and your story. Today is the day Jesus can become the hero of your story.

If today is your day, if you are reading this and coming to

realize that you have never expressed your need for Jesus to save you from your sins and give you a new start—a new heart, a new life, a new power, and a new future—I urge you respond to his call right now. Acknowledge to God that you have sinned and fallen short of living a life of obedience to him. If you believe that Jesus died for you on the cross, then state that out loud in prayer to God right now. Surrender your life to Jesus as the one you want to save you (Savior) and the one you want to lead you (Lord). Then ask him to fill you with his Spirit to enable you to live a new life with his power and to lead you every day to serve him as your King

By the way, if you just came to believe in and receive Jesus as your Savior and Lord, you might want to reread this book. I'm not saying that because I want you to read my book twice. I'm saying that because you will read it differently now. The truths of Jesus will be more amazing to you and more transforming in your life because you are new and you have God's Spirit to guide you.

Reflect and Pray

I have mentioned three ways I encourage people to share their stories. In every case, I urge those who are listening to reflect on what they hear. I often ask a question like this: "Do you have any other questions for Jill?" This question provides a way for me to learn what our group heard and discovered. It also creates an opportunity for those more developed in gospel fluency to ask additional questions to draw out the heart. Often, a person has not made Jesus the hero of his story because he is parroting what he has heard others do. Those who are mature in the gospel often ask questions that help the person make much of Jesus.

For instance, they might ask, "So, how did you come to know what God was like through Jesus?" I remember that when Nikki shared her story in our group, it was apparent that her view of a father was not great, but she longed for the love of a man nonetheless. One of the group members asked her, "Nikki, now that you have come to know God loves you through Jesus, how has that changed you view of *father*?" I've heard others say, "What does Jesus mean to you now?" or, "How has Jesus's death on the cross for your sins changed how you look at yourself now?" There are many questions we can ask. In all of them, we are helping people learn to make Jesus the hero of their stories.

Often, he isn't their hero. Oh, they might call themselves Christians, but when they tell their stories, it soon becomes clear that they don't know Jesus at all. Don't be surprised; this is more common than you think. When this happens, ask them if they've ever come to know Jesus. Ask them what he means to them. Invite them to share what they believe about him. Your growth in gospel fluency may start by sharing the gospel with someone in your group who has never come to believe in Jesus.

After we hear a person's story, I like to gather the group around the person, lay hands on her if she is OK with that, and pray, giving thanks to God for the work of Jesus in her life.

The story should declare Jesus to be the hero, and then we should give thanks in prayer to Jesus for being the hero of our stories.

Gospel fluency is developed both in sharing our stories and in thanking the one who wrote them.

PART 5

THE GOSPEL TO OTHERS

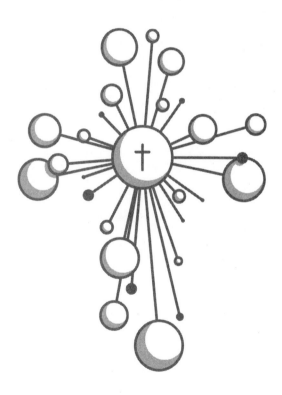

13

LISTEN AND LEARN

I recently observed a conversation a few Christians were having with a man who has yet to come to faith in Jesus. It was amazing to me, and saddening, to watch the Christians missing the point of this man's struggle and questions. It seemed those speaking to him were more concerned about convincing him they were right than about listening to his heart. As a result, he walked away without any good news about Jesus, becoming even more convinced that this "religion" wasn't for him.

It's not for me either—at least, not what I saw in that conversation.

We can do better. We *must* do better. We're talking about people's souls!

And we're representing Jesus.

Helping people come to know the love of Jesus is the most important thing there is, and Jesus's love for us compels us to love people better. If we don't, the good news that people need gets muffled by our religious pride.

Proverbs 20:5 says, "The purpose in a man's heart is like deep water, but a man of understanding will draw it out." We need to become people of understanding—people who seek to understand others before we expect them to understand us and what we believe. We need to learn how to ask more questions and draw out what is deep inside people's souls. We need to learn to slow down and listen closely to the longings of their hearts. We need to learn their stories. In short, we need to care more about winning people to Jesus than about winning arguments.

Gospel fluency isn't just about talking. It's about listening as well. This requires love, patience, and wisdom.

Drawing Out the Heart

Jesus was so good at this.

Whenever I consider how I can grow in being a person of understanding who listens well, I think of Jesus with the Samaritan woman at the well.[1]

It was high noon, when the sun was at its hottest. There was a reason this woman was getting her water at this time. She chose a time when no one else would be at the well. Nobody went there in the heat of the day. But she probably wanted to avoid running into one of the wives of the men with whom she had been sexually involved. She had had five husbands, and the man she was then involved with was not her husband.

However, Jesus didn't start with where she was wrong. He actually started in a humble posture of receiving from her.

---

1. This story is found in John 4.

He asked her for water, and she poured out her soul.

I've found that starting with a posture of humility, standing in a place of need and having a heart that is willing not only to give answers but also to receive insight, creates a welcoming place for people to open their hearts. The more open we are to listen and learn, the more likely people are to be open as well.

If you look at the story closely, you discover that Jesus continued to make very short, provocative statements that invited more conversation. He was drawing out, little by little, the longing of her soul.

He's a master at drawing out the heart.

You notice this if you read the Gospels. Jesus regularly said just enough to invite further probing or create intrigue. He also loved to ask questions so that the overflow of the heart (belief) would spill out of a person's mouth (words).

I'm amazed at how often well-intentioned Christians overwhelm people with a barrage of words. We go on and on about what we believe and what they should believe, assuming we know what others think, believe, or need. I often find that we are giving answers to questions people are not even asking or cramming information into hearts that are longing for love, not just facts.

We fail to listen. We fail to draw out the heart. And we miss opportunities to really love people and share the love of God with them. They also miss out on getting to hear what's going on in their own hearts. I have found that when people, including myself, are invited to say out loud what they believe, they come to realize something is wrong.

This is why counseling is a busy enterprise. People have no one to listen to them. They need to speak out loud what is going on in their hearts, and the only way some can do so is by paying a counselor to listen. I'm all for counseling, but I've spoken with many counselors, and most of them agree that if

God's people would slow down, close their mouths, open their ears, and listen, many people wouldn't need to see counselors.

Jesus slows down, draws out the heart, and listens.

As he did this at the well, the Samaritan woman's heart spilled out. And as it did, he guided her in a process of confession—not just of her behaviors, but also of her beliefs. She had been looking for love in all the wrong places and had clearly misunderstood God and how he interacts with humans. As Jesus engaged and listened, he was able to show her how he could provide what she most thirsted for. He could lead her to a well that would never run dry, providing an unending supply of soul water. *He* was the water that would deeply satisfy her soul.

The love she was looking for was standing right in front of her. And the God she should worship would go with her wherever she went. He wasn't on this mountain or that. He said he wants to come to human hearts like an unending stream of water that refreshes the soul.

She believed Jesus, and then went to tell her whole village about him. That's what you want to do with good news—share it with others. When people really grasp the good news of Jesus, satisfying the deep longings of their souls, it's hard for them to keep it to themselves.

Talk Less, Listen More

As we are changed by the gospel, we want to share how the gospel has changed us. It's a great thing to do so. In fact, one of the keys to growing in gospel fluency is to regularly share what Jesus has done or is doing in our lives with others. Our stories are powerful demonstrations of the gospel's power to save.

However, if we don't also listen, we tend to share the good news of Jesus in a way that applies primarily to our lives, the way it was good news to *us*, but fails to address the situations others are facing. We can become proclaimers of the good news while remaining ignorant of the ways in which others need to hear it. This doesn't negate how good the news of Jesus is at all. However, if we read the rest of the story of Jesus's encounter with the Samaritan woman, we find that while her testimony created intrigue, the people in the village had to meet Jesus for themselves. It wasn't enough for her just to share her story. They had to get to Jesus as well.

So she brought them to him.

Our job is to testify to Jesus's work in our lives while also listening closely to others so we know how to bring the truths of Jesus to bear on the longings of their hearts. We need to bring them to Jesus so he can meet *their* unique needs and fulfill *their* personal longings.

In order to do this, we have to slow down, quiet our souls, ask good questions to draw out the hearts of others, and *listen*.

Francis Schaeffer said, "If I have only an hour with someone, I will spend the first fifty-five minutes asking them questions and finding out what is troubling their heart and mind, and then in the last five minutes I will share something of the truth."[2]

My regular counsel to Christians these days is to spend more time listening than talking if they want to be able to share the gospel of Jesus in a way that meaningfully speaks to the hearts of others.

We were created by God to find our greatest satisfaction and fulfillment in him. Every human is hungry for God. Everyone has eternity written on their hearts, producing a longing for something—someone—better, more significant, and eternal. This is a longing for God (Eccl. 3:11). The cry of every heart—the native tongue of our souls—is for better, not for worse; for

---

2. Cited in Jerram Barrs, introduction to Francis A. Schaeffer, *He Is There and He Is Not Silent*, 30th Anniversary Edition (Wheaton, IL: Tyndale House, 2001), xviii.

the eternal, not for the temporal; for healing, redemption, and restoration. And only Jesus can bring this about.

We all long for Jesus Christ. Everyone is seeking him, even if they don't know it.

They are looking for something to fulfill their longings and satisfy their thirst.

However, they are looking in the wrong places. They are going to the wrong wells to try to draw soul water. They need to look to Jesus. But they will not come to see how he can quench their thirst if we don't take the time to listen.

And as we listen, with the help of the Holy Spirit, we can discern the longings of their hearts, the brokenness of their souls, and the emptiness of their spirits. And then, we must be prepared to show how Jesus can meet them at the well with soul-quenching water—himself.

Listening Up

Whenever I am engaging in a conversation with someone, I ask the Holy Spirit to help me. He is called "the Helper," after all (John 14:26).

"Help me slow down," I pray. "Help me to trust you are working here in the silence. Help me to listen well—to them and to you."

In some Bible versions, "Helper" is translated as "Counselor." So I ask the Spirit to give me the ability to hear the longings of the heart as I listen. I invite him to be the primary counselor in the midst of our time. I ask him to give me ears to hear what the real issues are, and then provide me with wisdom as to how to share the truths of Jesus in such a way that they will be good news to the other person.

Recently, on a plane, I happened to sit next to a woman who was very troubled. I didn't know this at first because she looked polished and seemed pleasant in her greeting. Oftentimes when I travel, I ask God if the time on the plane is for me to be alone for my work or rest, or if he wants me to engage in a redemptive conversation. The answer is usually fairly obvious within minutes of takeoff. In this case, he wanted me to have a conversation.

I asked the woman, "So, are you leaving home or headed home?"

She replied: "Well, both, I guess. I live in Seattle, but I'm flying to the place that was supposed to be my new home. My husband and boys are there now. It's a little complicated."

"Help me, Spirit," I prayed. "Help me to listen well."

She continued: "We couldn't all move at the same time because I had to stay back to work for a while longer in Seattle. However, now we're getting a divorce, so I will be staying in Seattle. I'm just going to see my sons and sign divorce papers and head back home."

I asked what had happened and she continued to open up. I continued to pray and listen to both her and the Spirit (what I call listening *up*). The story just poured out of her mouth. The dam had been ready to burst for some time.

I have found that when you make space for others, and they really believe you care, they are eager to open up and pour out their hearts. I don't believe this is just a technique, by the way. I'm convinced more and more that God's Spirit is at work ahead of us, and as we depend on him, he produces the fruit of love, joy, peace, patience, kindness, goodness, faithfulness, gentleness, and self-control in our lives (Gal. 5:22–25). I'm increasingly convinced that people can sense something is different about us. So they are often more prone to share when they experience the Spirit's presence and his fruit in our lives.

The woman on the plane went on to describe how she had had an affair and how her husband, in his anger, had done everything he could to destroy her image on Facebook, turning all their friends against her. He had succeeded in turning her sons against her as well. She was terribly embarrassed, broken, and demoralized. I listened for quite some time, and it became clear to me that she was sorry for what she had done and regretted the pain and shame it had brought on her and her family. Not only did she feel bad, but she was being crushed by the weight of it. The guilt and the shame were too much to bear. And she was deeply burdened by her husband's anger and her sons' pain.

Listen for the longing, listen for the pain, listen for the need for Jesus.

She wanted to make things right. She wanted forgiveness, healing, and reconciliation.

Jesus had good news for her.

At one point, she stopped and said: "You sure are nice. You've been listening to me go on and on about my life, and I've hardly asked you about yours. You're just so easy to talk to. Who are you?" She seemed surprised that a stranger would listen and show he cared.

I then explained to her who I was and, most importantly, who I knew. I let her know that I know and love Jesus, and that Jesus cared and was listening to her as well. She then shared how she had never been into religion, but recently she had been seeking and checking out some churches in our area. She knew she needed help and was reaching out.

As I said above, I am more and more convinced that the Holy Spirit goes ahead of us, preparing people for conversations like this. This growing confidence in God as the one who saves has freed me from the pressure to be the savior for people. Our job is to be present, filled with the Spirit, and ready to listen, then open to speak as the Spirit leads.

I shared with the woman that she was feeling shame and guilt because of her sin and her subsequent attempts to deal with it. I shared with her the story of Adam and Eve, and how they tried to deal with their sin. I continued to show her how it led them to blame each other and brought destruction in their relationships.

"You and your husband both experientially know the pain of sin," I said. "And because sin is ultimately a violation against God, the giver of life, and his ways, which protect and promote life, you are both looking for someone to pay the penalty for that violation. The Bible calls this payment 'atonement.' We all know someone should pay for sin. So when we sin or are sinned against, we look for someone or something to atone for it. If we look to ourselves, we self-loathe and hate, which is shame and guilt having its way in us. If we look to blame others, we become bitter and we hate them, wanting them to pay. In either case, the sin never really is dealt with. It doesn't go away. Instead, it produces more destruction. In many cases, we try to earn our own atonement by trying to be better, work harder, or promise never to do it again. But that leads to other forms of destruction, such as perfectionism, workaholism, manipulation, and pride, or devastation and depression when we fail.

"What you need," I continued, "is one who can truly atone for your sin. You need someone who can handle the weight of sin, forgive you of your sin, and set you free from it, so that it no longer defines you. You need Jesus."

I then went on to describe how Jesus willingly went to the cross to take her sin on himself. I shared how he was willing to be publicly shamed for her so that she not only could be forgiven but also clothed in his righteousness and freed from guilt and shame.

"You will never be able to do enough to remove your guilt and cover your shame through your own efforts," I said. "Only Jesus can do that for you. And your husband hates you because he is also looking for atonement for your sin. That makes sense if he doesn't know Jesus. He doesn't have another place to go to. Until he meets Jesus, he will continue to expect you to pay for what you've done. And if you don't go to Jesus for forgiveness, you will keep carrying both the weight of your sin and your husband's hatred of you for it. You can be forgiven by going to Jesus in faith and receiving his forgiveness. And every time you are reminded of your sin and your husband's rage, you can redirect that in your heart to Jesus. Let Jesus take the guilt, the shame. And ask him to carry the weight of your husband's hatred toward you. You can't handle it. But Jesus can and did at the cross. He died to remove it and to heal you of its scars."

We went on and on about how the gospel brings forgiveness, healing, hope, and even love for those we've hurt or been hurt by.

At the end, she said: "I feel like I got a free counseling session with God just now. I'm convinced he set up our seating arrangements for this flight."

I agreed. He does that kind of thing.

He wants to do that through you as well, if you will set aside your self, your assumptions, and your need to be heard or be right, and just listen. Listen to the people God has put into your life and listen to what the Spirit has to say. Then you will know how to speak the gospel to the deep longings of people's souls.

Many are going to other wells to find water.

Let's be willing to slow down in order to lovingly show them how Jesus is standing ready to uniquely satisfy their thirst.

Learn Their Stories

As you grow in listening to people's longings, also learn to listen for their overarching stories. In the last chapter, I described how we can share our stories, making Jesus the hero. If we are going to speak the gospel fluently to the hearts of others, we need to listen for the dominant storylines under which others live their lives. What are their gospel stories? Who's their hero?

Everyone has a gospel story he or she believes. It may not be the gospel of the kingdom of God—the good news of Jesus Christ—but it is a gospel narrative nonetheless. The gospel narrative everyone believes includes the storyline of Creation, Fall, Redemption, and New Creation. Oh, they wouldn't necessarily use those words, but since eternity is written on their hearts, they are wired by God with this storyline.

If you pay attention, you will see that this is the storyline of every great novel, play, and movie. It spills out of our songs and poems. It jumps out of our television screens in sitcoms, dramas, and even commercials. Gospel-fluent ears learn to listen to where the storylines of our friends and our culture agree and disagree with the true story of God.

So how does this work?

Let's look at the fundamental questions or longings in each movement of the story in light of people God has put in our lives. Get familiar with them, and then, as you listen to people, listen for their answers to the questions:

Creation: In what do they find their *identity* or sense of purpose and significance?

Fall: Whom or what is the fundamental *problem* they blame for the things that are broken in their lives?

Redemption: Whom or what are they looking to as their *savior* to rescue or deliver them?

New Creation: What does transformation look like and what is their ultimate *hope* for the future?

One day, a friend called and told me he had lost his job. He was not a believer in Jesus, but he was open to talking about the things of the heart. He asked if we could get together for lunch to talk about how he was doing.

So there we were at one of our favorite Mexican restaurants in Tacoma. I asked him how he was doing.

"Not well," he responded.

I started to reply, "I can understand why, what with losing your job and worrying about bills and all that." But I felt prompted by the Spirit: "Ask why. Don't assume. Listen."

"Why are you not doing well?" I asked.

"Well, you would think it was because I lost my job and was worried about paying the bills, feeding the family."

"Well, yes," I thought, "that's what I would think."

"That's not it, though," he said. "The reason I'm not doing well is because I'm not really sure who I am anymore."

I felt as if the Spirit prompted me again: "Ask another question."

So I asked, "What do you mean?"

"Well," he continued, "I'm beginning to see that my job was my identity. And without it, I'm not sure who I am anymore."

"I can see that," I shared. "I went through a similar crisis a few years back. I had been looking to my job or my job performance to find my sense of identity and significance. I think we all do that in different ways with different things in life."

"Yeah, I think you're right. The thing that's got me a bit is that even though I know I could get another job, I could lose it just like this one. There's no guarantee. I think that's what's shaking me up the most. None of this is stable or dependable."

"I can understand that," I said. I let some time pass, then I said: "I know you grew up on a ranch in Montana. But I don't know if I've ever heard much about what it was like for you growing up there. Would you mind sharing with me more about what your life was like growing up?"

"Sure," he said. "My dad was a rancher, so I didn't really see him much. In fact, I hardly spent time with him. He did eat dinner with us when he wasn't driving cattle. I knew that when I turned eighteen I would start working with him on the ranch, but he died when I was sixteen."

I'll never forget that moment. It was as if the Holy Spirit was yelling in my ear: "Did you hear that? He lost his dad. He was planning on working for his dad to get to him through work, and then, through his work, feel the approval and love of a father. But his dad died before that could happen. Now he is looking to his work to get approval, and he's lost that too."

What was his creation narrative? "My identity is in my job because I'm looking for approval and love from my dad."

What was his fall narrative? "My dad died and I lost my job. And even though I could get another job, I could lose it as well. Nothing is dependable. Nothing lasts. We lose dads and jobs."

What was his redemption narrative? "I need a dad who will love me and a job well done."

What was his new creation narrative? "I want a dad who won't die and will be proud of my work."

Do you see how the gospel has great news for my friend? With the Spirit's help, I did. So I gave it to him.

"You want a good thing. You want the love of a father who will never leave you. And you want to do good work for him so that he will be pleased with you. I want to let you know that there is a Father who wants to be a perfect Dad for you. That's God. He loves you and will never die. In fact, he sent his Son, Jesus, to come and work on your behalf. He did a perfect job living the human life so that he could give you his perfection in exchange for your failures—your sin. Jesus died on the cross to forgive you and to make you perfectly acceptable and loved by God the Father. Through faith in Jesus, you are forgiven and loved by God, who is a perfect Dad for you. And Jesus rose again on the third day so that death wouldn't have the final say. Death is defeated, and the job was done perfectly so that you can have the love and acceptance of God your Father forever. Through faith in Jesus, you get a loving Father who will never die and a work that will never fail for you."

"I've never heard anything like that before," he said. "I grew up Lutheran, but never heard about Jesus that way before."

He needed the good news of Jesus shared as good news for his pain and longing.

My friend has yet to come to faith in Jesus, but he has a new view of God as Father and a job well done because of Jesus. I pray he believes someday.

Remember, we don't save people. God does. We listen and learn, and then we love and share Jesus.

14

SHOW AND TELL

In the true story, we learn that God has always intended to have a visible representation of himself on the earth. Adam and Eve failed. Then Israel failed. But Jesus did not. He is the true image of God—the fullness of deity in bodily form. Now, we, the church, are his body, the means by which he intends to fill every place with his embodied presence through our physical bodies (Eph. 1:22–23). We were not just saved *from* sin, Satan, and death. We were also saved *for* his purposes here and now.

Saved *from* and saved *for*.

We were saved by the power of God for the purposes of God, so that God might be made known and Jesus might be glorified. We are God's *display* people, showing the world what he is like. We are also his *declaration* people, who declare who God is and what he has done by proclaiming the gospel.

Peter says to God's people scattered throughout Asia Minor (modern-day Turkey), "But you are a chosen race, a royal priesthood, a holy nation, a people for his own possession, that you may proclaim the excellencies of him who called you out of darkness into his marvelous light" (1 Pet. 2:9). Then, in verse 12, he adds, "Keep your conduct among the Gentiles honorable, so that when they speak against you as evildoers, they may *see your good deeds* and *glorify God* on the day of visitation."

They were called to live as God's chosen people who loved others like family, just as God the Father had loved them while they were still his enemies. They were his royal priesthood, sent into the world by the Spirit to help people be reconciled to God and to one another through Jesus. And they were a holy nation, called to display what life can be like when Jesus is King.

So are we. This is our identity. This is our calling.

Show the world the love of the Father, the healing and reconciling power of the Spirit, and the sacrificial servanthood of the Son in how you live.

Show the world what God is like.

Peter continues to describe the kind of life they were to live as God's display people, and afterward, in 1 Peter 3:14–15, he says: "But even if you should suffer for righteousness' sake, you will be blessed. Have no fear of them, nor be troubled, but in your hearts honor Christ the Lord as holy, always being prepared to make a defense to anyone who asks you for a reason for the hope that is in you; yet do it with gentleness and respect."

Peter knows that not everyone will receive them or respond to them well. They may suffer for living God-displaying, God-glorifying lives. Some may reject and persecute them, while others may be led to give thanks and praise to God for them. Either way, Peter calls them to live a life that flows from the gospel. And, as a result, Peter wants them to be prepared to give the gospel—to give Jesus—as the reason why they do what they do. In other words, Peter is calling them to live a life that demands a gospel explanation—a life that makes no sense without sharing the truths about Jesus to explain why they do what they do. When people ask, God's people are to give them Jesus.

Display the truths of Jesus in your life and declare the truths of Jesus with your lips.

Show and tell.

Display

It has been said that behavior is more caught than taught. Every parent knows this to be true. Our children more often reflect what we do in front of them than what we say to them.

The display of our lives is definitely more convincing than the declaration of our lips. In fact, if we say one thing and do another, our doing often trumps what we say in people's minds.

So what are we displaying to the world?

From time to time, I've led groups to embrace the practice of being a gospel display through an activity I call "Gospel Metaphors." I encourage the group members to think about the gospel and what we come to know about God through Jesus's work. Then I invite them to share the titles, attributes, and activities of God that we see in Jesus.

Advocate. Sacrifice. Healer. Forgiver. Counselor. Prince of Peace. Restorer. Redeemer. The list could go on and on.

While people are sharing, I write the words down on a whiteboard or poster-sized Post-it note.

Then I pick one. If I choose *Restorer*, I say: "We have been blessed to be a blessing. God has shown us what he is like by what he has done for us. Now we get to show the world what he is like by what we do for them. So, how might we show how

God brings restoration through Jesus in our neighborhood or community?"

Some of the responses have been:

- "Well, we could walk the neighborhood together in prayer, asking the Spirit to show us what is broken and needs repair, then offer to repair it."
- "We could lead a study for the community on how to deal with conflict in our relationships."
- "What if we start with everyone in our group? Do we have brokenness that needs to be dealt with? How are our relationships doing? How are our hearts doing? Let's make sure we are experiencing restoration ourselves first."

Often, many suggestions are given. And I usually select a few additional attributes or titles and ask how we could provide pictures of what God is like in those ways.

The apostle Paul said we are like living letters displaying the work of God to the world—gospel metaphors.

As a result of an exercise such as this, I've witnessed fences repaired (*Restorer*); houses remodeled to make more space for people in need of places to stay (*Hospitable*); an empty lot that was used for drug and sex trafficking transformed into a community garden (*Redeemer*); debts paid off (*Forgiver*); college tuition raised (*Provider*); fatherless children cared for by men (*Father to the fatherless*); and many other displays of the character of God. Small and big activities alike can display what God is like, as we've come to know him in the gospel.

We are blessed by God to bless others. Physical displays of what God is like show his glory in tangible form.

Every time I describe this idea, I am reminded of a brunch Jayne and I hosted with some members of our missional community one Sunday morning at our house. Many of our neighbors who didn't attend church gatherings were with us, and the conversation started to steer toward what was good and bad about our neighborhood. At one point, someone brought up the man who lived on the opposite corner from our house. He had found a way to get a special "Parking by permit only" sign put in front of his home. We lived in the city, where most people didn't have driveways, and parking was hard to come by. The problem was that there was no way for anyone else to get a permit. It seems he had some connections. The other problem was that there was no lighting by the sign, and a large tree limb hung in front of it, making it hard for drivers looking for parking spots to see the sign.

Of course, we all knew not to park there, but our friends from outside the neighborhood often were not aware—until they went out to their cars and found notes glued to their windshields. The notes said: "Can't you read? It's obvious you can't or you would not have been so dumb as to park here." Then the notes went on to describe what would happen if they parked there again. It was horrible! And many didn't know how to get the notes off their windshields without damaging the glass.

Not surprisingly, the conversation soon turned so negative that one person said: "I know he was in the military. That man is a trained killer. I wouldn't be surprised if there weren't bodies buried in the cement in his basement!"

I had to stop it.

"Hey, everyone, I think that's probably enough," I said. "Since he's not here to defend himself, it might be better that we stop." He wasn't present because he wasn't a friend of anyone in the room, but the main reason was because he was overseeing a local church's worship gathering that morning. The fact that everyone knew he was a pastor didn't help in our mission of representing Jesus to the neighbors in that room. They had a very poor image of Christians as a result of his behavior.

I continued: "Besides, I don't think any of us really know

him that well. Jayne and I are just getting to know him. We just had him over for dinner this past Friday night, and we found him to be a very nice man."

As I said that, I could see the surprise on their faces and feel their skepticism. People were likely thinking: "What in the world are you doing, Jeff? Why would you befriend that man?"

"I'm not sure if you know his story, but as we learned more about him, it helped me understand why he does what he does. Please hear me, I don't think what he is doing is good. It's wrong for sure. But I've found that hurt people hurt people. And he has been really hurt throughout his life. Again, I won't justify what he has done. I don't like it either. But since he's not here for us to talk to, maybe we shouldn't talk about him anymore. In fact, I am praying for a day when he will be with us, asking us to forgive him for what he has done to hurt so many of us."

I became an advocate for a man who couldn't advocate for himself. I became an advocate for a man who deserved the judgment of that room. I did what God does for me in Jesus Christ.

Jesus is our Advocate. He is currently advocating for me in a place I cannot be—before God the Father. And though I deserve condemnation for my sin, he speaks a better word of commendation over me as a son of God.

We are called to be gospel pictures, gospel metaphors. In advocating for this man, I was trying to present a picture of God.

I finished and the conversation shifted. I could tell some felt uncomfortable and others were just confused.

Amy was one of them. She lived next door to this man and had become a good friend of ours over the years, but she hadn't trusted Jesus. She pulled me aside the next day and asked: "What were you thinking yesterday, Jeff? Everyone knows how evil he is. We've all been treated terribly by him. I don't get it. Why would you do that?"

Declare

I've found that when we live our lives intentionally as display people, we get plenty of opportunities to talk about why we do it. Lives full of grace and love; schedules rearranged to make space to listen and serve; budgets adjusted to feed and care for people; or words spoken to protect and build up all demand explanations. These things really don't make sense apart from the gospel.

Yet in our explanations to others, we so often forget to give them Jesus.

In his book *Spiritual Disciplines for the Christian Life*, Donald Whitney writes:

> I heard the story of a man who became a Christian during an evangelistic emphasis in a city in the Pacific Northwest. When the man told his boss about it, his employer responded with: "That's great! I am a Christian and have been praying for you for years!"
>
> But the new believer was crestfallen. "Why didn't you ever tell me you were a Christian? You were the very reason I have not been interested in the gospel all these years."
>
> "How can that be?" the boss wondered. "I have done my very best to live the Christian life around you."
>
> "That's the point," explained the employee. "You lived such a model life without telling me it was Christ who made the difference, I convinced myself that if you could live such a good and happy life without Christ, then I could too."[1]

I wonder how often our good, moral lives, disconnected from any gospel explanation, convince people they don't need Jesus?

We need to do more than just be nice. We need to tell them why we live as we do.

---

1. Donald S. Whitney, *Spiritual Disciplines for the Christian Life*, revised and updated edition (Wheaton, IL: Tyndale House, 2014), 133.

Paul says to the church in Rome, "How then will they call on him in whom they have not believed? And how are they to believe in him of whom they have never heard? And how are they to hear without someone preaching? And how are they to preach unless they are sent? As it is written, "How beautiful are the feet of those who preach the good news!" (Rom. 10:14–15). The feet that run to carry our hands and faces that display the gospel must also bring along mouths ready to declare the gospel.

I was speaking recently at a large church in Texas. One part of my message was about being display people and the other part was about being declaration people. In fact, I shared the above story from Whitney's book and made it very clear that we must tell people that Jesus is the reason we do what we do. "Let's not rob Jesus of the credit," I said. "Let's not steal away his glory."

Afterward, a very nice woman complimented me on the message and went on to describe how she and her husband had been trying to love their neighbors. She shared how complex the relationships within their cul-de-sac had become, as most of the neighbors didn't like or trust one another. However, she and her husband loved and served everyone regardless. I was encouraged by all the ways they were seeking to love their neighbors. Then she told me that one of her neighbors had come to her and said: "I don't understand why you do it. Why are you so kind to that man [a neighbor no one liked]?" I expected her to excitedly tell me how she had done what I had just taught and had given Jesus as the reason for the hope that she had— the gospel explanation for the life she lived. Instead, she said: "Well, I just told her: 'We're just being kind. It's not hard to be kind.'" I stood looking at her for a moment. I think my jaw dropped, making my wonderment a little too conspicuous, and she looked slightly uncomfortable.

"That's what you told her?" I asked. "Anything else?" I wanted to give her space for a further explanation.

"No, that's it," she said. "'It's not hard to be kind' is what I said."

I couldn't leave it at that, so I gently encouraged her: "Next time I hope you'll share how Jesus has changed you. Maybe say something like: 'Well, God has been so loving to us. When we were the unlovable ones, he sent his Son, Jesus, to die on the cross for our sins. We love our neighbors like this because he loved us first.'"

I went on to say: "Your neighborhood will always be a broken place if your neighbors don't come to know Jesus and the Father's love for them personally. Kindness alone doesn't change neighborhoods. Jesus does. It's great that they experience his kindness and grace in your actions, but until they hear it is because of Jesus and are changed by Jesus themselves, you will be the only ones in the cul-de-sac who have his resources to love others with. I can imagine you would love for everyone to know his love, correct?"

She said, "Yes, of course!"

"Well," I asked, "can I encourage you to share Jesus as the reason for your kindness next time?"

I hope she does. And I hope you do when you have opportunities.

When we live Jesus-like lives but don't share the reason we can and do, we rob Jesus of his glory. He deserves the credit for what we do, not us.

Overcoming Our Hesitations

I understand that we often experience fear or insecurity when opportunities like these come up. I know that it's not easy for many of us to share Jesus with others.

I believe there are many reasons for this. First, as I said

in chapter 7, we are in a spiritual battle, so the enemy of our souls tries everything possible to keep us from speaking about Jesus. He can intimidate us to remain silent lest we be mocked or accused. Second, many of us love what people think of us more than we love people. So in our fear of rejection, we keep our mouths shut. I pray you will love people more than their opinions of you. Third, most Christians have never tried to share their gospel hope, and therefore have never experienced the Spirit of God giving them words and boldness. When you do step out in faith, it's amazing how he gives you what you need. Fourth, many Christians just don't know the gospel very well or, if they do, don't practice sharing it with other believers very often. They aren't gospel fluent.

I pray that this book has given you a better knowledge of the gospel and some tools for how to grow in your gospel fluency.

But the fifth reason for our silence is possibly the most concerning. I have found that most Christians don't really believe that their neighbors, friends, and family members will spend eternity apart from God if they don't have faith in Jesus. Judgment is coming. Hell is real. And apart from faith in Jesus Christ, people will miss out on enjoying life with God forever.

It is so important that we give people the good news of Jesus. It's not our job to get them to believe it. That's the Spirit's job. We are called to live lives that demand gospel explanations and, when we have the opportunities, to give people Jesus as the answer for our hope. We might show how Jesus is better than what they have been trusting in. Maybe we listen to their stories and help them find hope, healing, and redemption by filling in the gaps with the true story. Or perhaps, just by listening, we discover their deeper longings and show how Jesus can do for them what nothing and no one else can. Maybe, like Jayne, they need someone to help them see that the fruit of their lives is connected to the roots of their faith, and the time has come for them to see that they can place their faith in far better roots. Whatever the means, whatever the method, they need to hear about Jesus and the good news of the gospel.

Let's go back to my neighbor's interrogation: "What were you thinking yesterday, Jeff? Why would you do that?"

"Amy," I began, "I did that because he needed an advocate. He wasn't in the room and couldn't defend himself. As I said, I know what he has done is wrong, but I've learned to advocate for people, even if they are wrong, because of what God has done for me. Right now, I have Jesus Christ as my Advocate before God the Father in heaven. I have sinned. I have done what is wrong, and I deserve death for it. However, Jesus died for my sins on the cross and rose again from the dead. He was then raised up and seated next to God the Father, where he is constantly advocating for me. He is speaking far better words about me than I could ever deserve! He is representing me in a place I don't deserve to be. But because he is, I can have a relationship with God that isn't just for now, but forever. I'm an advocate because he is an Advocate for me."

"I just don't get you, Jeff!" she responded.

"I know, but I hope one day you will get Jesus," I replied.

She said: "I don't know about that. I don't think I'll ever believe."

I can pray, display, and declare, but I can't save.

That's God's job. So I will keep on listening, loving, blessing, sharing, and praying.

15

GROW IN LOVE AND WISDOM

Well, we're coming to the end. I hope that, through this book, you've gained more knowledge about the grace, mercy, and kindness of God through the good news of Jesus. I also pray you've become more fluent in speaking the gospel and listening with gospel ears. However, my greatest hope is that you love Jesus more now than when you started reading. Gospel fluency won't happen *through* you until it happens *to* you. You talk most about what you love most. I pray that I have helped you love Jesus more.

I also pray your love for people has grown.

One of my concerns is that the tools and ideas in this book will become a hammer instead of a healing balm. The tendency of many well-intentioned people is to take a tool meant for love and instead hurt people with it by handling it without gentleness and care. We sometimes learn new truths and then think that if we just speak the truth to one another, that will be enough. But remember, Paul clarifies that we are called to speak the truth to one another *in love* (Eph. 4:15).

In another place, while instructing the church in Corinth on how to handle the truths he had given them, as well as the gifts God had given them, Paul says: "If I speak in the tongues of men and of angels, but have not love, I am a noisy gong or a clanging cymbal. And if I have prophetic powers, and understand all mysteries and all knowledge, and if I have all faith, so as to remove mountains, but have not love, I am nothing. If I give away all I have, and if I deliver up my body to be burned, but have not love, I gain nothing" (1 Cor. 13:1–3).

We can have right knowledge of the gospel, faith in the gospel, power to proclaim the gospel, and all the tools in the world to creatively do so, but still lack love. And if that is the case, our proclamation will mean nothing. At the heart of the gospel is the love of God. And if we speak about the love of God without love for people, the noise of our lives will drown out the words coming from our lips.

A few years back, I met a young man who had a zeal for sharing the gospel. He would stand on a wooden block in the park and use a variety of means to engage a crowd to listen to him. Honestly, it often felt more like entrapment then evangelism. He used some clever methods to induce people to publicly admit how they had failed, then used their failure to perfectly keep the law to lead them to their need for grace. What I mean is that he would ask them if they had ever lied, stolen things, had lustful thoughts, or had hatred in their hearts for others. He would then describe how they had violated God's commands and assure them that all who do so have sinned. After this, he would share that the wages of sin is death, but the gift of God is eternal life through Jesus Christ our Lord (Rom. 6:23). He would explain the gospel further and then invite them to respond.

To be clear, I'm not necessarily criticizing this form of evangelism, though I do have some questions and concerns with some of the ways I've observed it done. In the case of this young man, my biggest concern with his method was his motive for sharing the gospel.

So I asked him why he did what he did. He told me he wanted to be able to stand before God one day and know that he was innocent of the blood of all the people with whom he could have shared the gospel. When he said this, I thought: "He doesn't love the people. He is doing this to save himself." His motive was self-justification, not love for the lost.

So I then asked him: "Do you know those people in the park? And do you love them?" The truth is that he couldn't really know them, and I'm not sure that he loved them either.

We went back and forth on our opinions regarding open-air evangelism, which is not my point in this story, but eventually I asked him, "Do you love your neighbors?" This caught him off guard a bit.

Finally he replied, "Well, not really."

"Do you know them?" I continued.

"No," he replied.

"Do you have people who don't know Jesus yet as friends?"

"Not really," he said again.

Hearing this, I responded, "I want to call you to know and love people, and then both show the love of Jesus to them and share it as well."

He took me up on it. He started to get to know and love his neighbors. I watched this young man grow significantly in love, grace, and gentleness. He also grew in boldness and faith.

He still shares the gospel, but he does it with a much more gracious, loving, and gentle heart. He is now a pastor of a church that is also growing in how to show and share the love of Jesus.

Do you love people? More specifically, do you love those who are different—who don't live like you or believe what you believe? If not, I want to encourage you to ask God to grant you his heart for people. Ask him to give you love for your neighbors, coworkers, family members, and friends. Invite him to fill your heart with his love and then ask him to enable you to feel what he feels for people.

Remember, God loved you while you were still a sinner—his enemy. Jesus suffered and died to forgive you of your sins, make you a child of God, and pour the love of God into your heart by his Spirit. So ask him to give you his heart for people.

If you do, be ready. You will find that his love is greater than you imagined and deeper than you know.

Of course, he will do it gradually. He knows what he's doing and will not crush you with the full weight of his heart. But if you ask, he *will* change you. He has changed me and is still changing me. The more I get to know the love of God, the more deeply burdened I become for the lost and broken in our community.

My heart is being captured by God's heart for people. Yours will be too if you will submit it to him.

The more I ask God to give me his heart for people, the more pain and passion I feel. I have more heart and heartbreak. I shed more tears and have more joy. I feel more sadness and exude more happiness. I observe more crying and I hear more laughter. I see depths of brokenness and watch miraculous healing. I have found that love is not all warm and fuzzy. It also hurts. But the more God's love flows into me, the more my love grows for him and others. As a result, the more careful, gentle, and wise I want to be.

This is because love is embodied in wisdom—which is really where I want to end.

Get Wisdom

Wisdom isn't just increased knowledge, because knowledge without grace leads to pride, and pride leads to destruction in our lives and the lives of others. Wisdom is knowledge applied so that we do the right thing, at the right time, with the right motive, in the right way.

Wisdom is gracious, loving, kind, and gentle.

When Peter charges the believers in Asia Minor to be prepared to give an answer for the hope that is in them—to give a gospel explanation for their godly lives—he says they should do it with gentleness and respect (1 Pet. 3:15). He then points to Jesus as the ultimate good news preacher (vv. 18–22).

Likewise, Paul says to the church in Colossae: "Walk in wisdom toward outsiders, making the best use of the time. Let your speech always be gracious, seasoned with salt, so that you may know how you ought to answer each person" (Col. 4:5–6). Wisdom is timely. Wisdom is gracious. Wisdom is seasoned with salt because it is healing, life-preserving, and taste-enhancing. It makes life better, not worse; fuller, not lesser; and more savory, not more sour.

Wisdom is a gift, and all who have it are a blessing. You can easily tell the difference between those who act in wisdom and those who do not. James says: "But the wisdom from above is first pure, then peaceable, gentle, open to reason, full of mercy and good fruits, impartial and sincere. And a harvest of righteousness is sown in peace by those who make peace" (James 3:17–18).

Remember King Solomon? He had one request: that God would make him wise. He got that, and everything else with it as well—likely because he asked for wisdom, not other things.

Wisdom brings with it a harvest of many blessings. As a result, people traveled great distances to hear the wisdom God gave Solomon.

I have met many people who reject the truths of the gospel, but who nonetheless want to stay around God's people to experience the fruit of the gospel.

When I was very young in my faith, I read James 1:5: "If any of you lacks wisdom, let him ask God, who gives generously to all without reproach, and it will be given him." I knew I lacked wisdom, so I started asking God for wisdom almost every day, sometimes several times a day. Before Jesus changed my life, before I knew to ask him for wisdom, I was impure, selfish, prideful, and angry. However, he changed my heart, gave me his love, purified my motives, and, as I daily asked for wisdom, increasingly made me wise. I know this is all due to his grace, not my work. However, I knew I needed help. I knew I lacked wisdom (in fact, I still do; I have so much more to receive from him). Since he had promised to give it to those who know they lack it and ask for it, I did.

Since then, I have found that friends, both Christian and non-Christian, seek me out for counsel. As a result, I get to share the gospel more often. Thus, I don't just have wisdom from God to share, I also see the fruit of wisdom in my life.

Wisdom for Manhood

Amy, my neighbor who questioned my advocacy of our troublesome fellow neighbor, was one of those friends. Though she continued to reject the gospel, we still interacted over many topics. One day she confided in me regarding the teenage boys at the school where she taught. She was part of a team implementing a new strategy for improving education in lower-income, inner-city schools. One of the problems the team members were facing was that the boys were terribly disrespectful and inappropriate in their actions toward the girls at Amy's school. Their behavior was becoming highly disruptive and making the school a bit unsafe.

At this school, 85 percent of the students didn't have fathers at home. So, needless to say, there were very few good male role models. Amy's team had decided to start a "Saturday school" as part of its strategy, and the theme of the next Saturday training was a healthy view of manhood. Amy asked me and a friend of mine if we would come and teach on manhood. I asked her why she choose us. She said she had watched my life and how I handled myself with Jayne, our children, and our neighbors. Plus, she had seen how I respected women. So she felt I was a good example and that I could articulate what I believed about manhood effectively.

I'm convinced it was because, over the years, God had graciously given me wisdom in this area, wisdom that could be both heard and seen.

So my friend and I got to spend half a day talking about manhood to a large group of teenage boys in a public school setting. What an incredible opportunity! We shared many principles and examples of manhood. Then, at one point, we asked the boys who they believed were the best examples of manhood and why. They cited Gandhi, Martin Luther King Jr., Michael Jordan, Malcolm X, President Obama, and many more. With each suggestion, we asked why they believed each man was great. It was good to hear them identify some very admirable traits in all of these men.

"Any more examples?" I asked.

Eventually, one boy said, "Jesus."

"Yes!" I thought. "I was hoping he would be brought up!"

When we asked him why he had picked Jesus as his example, the boy said: "Well, all the men mentioned so far stood up for something they believed in. Did good for a lot of people.

And some even died for what they believed in. But Jesus didn't just come and teach, serve, love, and stand up for what he believed in. He also willingly died for people. Some of these other men were killed, but Jesus chose to die. And he didn't just die for the people who were on his side. He died for people who were against them. He died on the cross for sinners—for wicked people. And he didn't just die for people back then. He died for us as well. He laid down his life to forgive us. He died to save us. As far as I'm concerned, Jesus is the greatest man who ever lived!"

That boy has some wisdom—not just because he said this, but also because of how he said it.

We were in that classroom with the opportunity to talk about Jesus because God had given us wisdom as well. That wisdom didn't just come from our education. It came from God.

Ultimately, God's wisdom came in the form of Jesus Christ. The apostle Paul says that Jesus is the wisdom of God (1 Cor. 1:24, 30). He is the true and better wisdom. He is also the means by which we *get* wisdom.

The book of Proverbs advises us that the wisest thing we can do is get wisdom (Prov. 4:5, 7). It also instructs us that in order to *get* wisdom, we need to get wisdom. In other words, we need to obtain wisdom to understand and apply wisdom. We can't make sense out of wisdom without the wisdom to do so.

How do we do this? How do we get wisdom to apply wisdom so we can show and tell the good news of Jesus graciously, lovingly, and gently?

We have to get Jesus.

If you want the wisdom of God but haven't yet received God's wisdom for you in Jesus Christ, I invite you to surrender to him now. Receive what he has done for you in his life, death, and resurrection. Ask him to forgive you of your sins;

cleanse you and make you clean; and come and dwell in you by his Spirit.

Maybe you believe you've already done that. Fine. However, don't neglect to ask God to keep giving you wisdom. You don't have enough yet. None of us does. We all need more wisdom from God to work through the situations, struggles, and opportunities that we face every day.

As James says, "If any of you lacks wisdom, let him ask God, who gives generously to all without reproach, and it will be given him."

Ask God for wisdom and he will give you Jesus.

And if you get Jesus, you will get everything you need for every part of your life. He is good news for the everyday stuff of life.

Don't put your confidence in your knowledge or skills. Don't just look to the principles or practices of this book—or any other book—to make you more effective. What you need, what I need, what we all need is Jesus. That's where wisdom begins. That's where wisdom ends.

That's the heart of this book.

If you get Jesus, you get wisdom.

Get wisdom from Jesus and you get everything else as well.

He is better than everything else, and if you have him, then you'll give him to others.

Conclusion

In my first book, *Saturate*, my hope was that people would catch a vision for gospel saturation so that every man, woman, and child might have a daily encounter with Jesus in word and deed through his people together on mission.

I wanted to see seeds planted that would produce the fruit of the gospel in people's lives, fruit that would then spill out into every person and place where God's people lived, worked, and played. I dreamed of a day—I still do—when nobody will be able to get away from the loving and powerful presence of God through his people, the church, because his people do not believe they *go* to church, but that they *are* the church. They believe God's presence is in them wherever they go so that everyone might see and hear the love of God everywhere and every day.

I knew this would never happen if God's people didn't learn how to speak the gospel fluently. We need to learn to speak it graciously, wisely, and lovingly into the everyday stuff of life if people are going to hear it every day. That is why I wrote this book. I know that the church desperately needs to grow in gospel fluency. We need to learn how to speak the truths of Jesus into the everyday stuff of life.

So you're done with the book and you're ready, right?

Wrong.

I know that reading a book will never make you gospel fluent, any more than reading a book on Spanish grammar, memorizing Spanish vocabulary, and learning Spanish culture will make you fluent in Spanish. It's necessary, but not sufficient. It doesn't end here.

You have to speak the gospel—a lot. You need to hear it. You must be immersed in it.

And you need to love it. You need to love the gospel.

So don't just put this book down and move on. Your training has just begun.

Start regularly rehearsing the truths about Jesus over and over again in your mind. Invite the Spirit of God to wash over your heart with the depths of his love as we see it in the truth of the gospel. Regularly take captive your thoughts to bring them into submission to what is true of Jesus and what is true of you if your life is in Jesus. Surround yourself with people who love Jesus and want to grow in speaking the truths of Jesus into the everyday stuff of life. Be with them a lot. And make sure you invite them to speak into your life and into your heart. Submit yourself to others who want to give you Jesus, not just another self-help technique. And make sure you give them Jesus as well. He is the hope of the world! He is the changer of hearts! He is the only name under heaven given to us by which we might be saved.

And as you speak Jesus to one another, do it with grace, wisdom, and love, all of which you can get from him in limitless supply. As you receive these gifts from him, give him credit for what he gives and what he does. Keep speaking Jesus, because you talk about what works—and Jesus *works*; the gospel *works*. Keep growing in your love for Jesus, because you talk most about what you love most. The gospel is the love of God that works because it is the power of God for salvation for all who believe. So don't be ashamed! Tell yourself. Tell your friends. Tell your family members. Tell everyone that you have good news for them—good news that will change them forever.

God loves them. Jesus lived, died, and rose again for them. Their lives—every single part—can be changed forever as a result. It's true for you as well. Don't forget it. There really isn't anything better to talk about than Jesus. There also isn't anything better for meeting our every need than Jesus.

So let's start learning together how to speak Jesus into the everyday stuff of life together, every day and everywhere. It starts now.

Gospel fluency class is now in session.

General Index

Scripture Index